PENGUIN LIBERTY

CLASSIC SUPREME COURT CASES

Corey Brettschneider is a professor of political science at Brown University, where he teaches constitutional law and politics, as well as a visiting professor of law at Fordham University School of Law. He has also been a visiting professor at Harvard Law School and the University of Chicago Law School. His writing has appeared in *The New York Times*, *Politico*, and *The Washington Post*. He is the author of *The Oath and the Office: A Guide to the Constitution for Future Presidents*, two books about constitutional law and civil liberties, and numerous articles published in academic journals and law reviews. His constitutional law casebook is widely used in classrooms throughout the United States. Brettschneider holds a PhD in politics from Princeton University and a JD from Stanford Law School.

Classic
SUPREME COURT CASES

A Selection

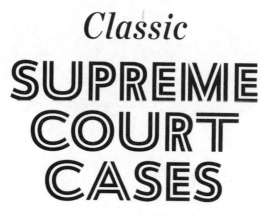

EDITED WITH AN INTRODUCTION BY
Corey Brettschneider

SERIES EDITOR
Corey Brettschneider

PENGUIN BOOKS

PENGUIN BOOKS
An imprint of Penguin Random House LLC
penguinrandomhouse.com

ISBN 9780143135135 (paperback)
ISBN 9780525506812 (ebook)

Printed in the United States of America
1st Printing

Book design by Daniel Lagin

Contents

Series Introduction by Corey Brettschneider   ix

Introduction by Corey Brettschneider   xxv

A Note on the Text   xxxiii

Classic SUPREME COURT CASES

Part I: ORIGINS OF JUDICIAL REVIEW   1

Calder v. Bull (1798)   3

Marbury v. Madison (1803)   10

Part II: EQUAL PROTECTION   23

Dred Scott v. Sandford (1857)   25

Yick Wo v. Hopkins (1886)   30

Chae Chan Ping v. United States (1889)   36

Plessy v. Ferguson (1896)   44

United States v. Wong Kim Ark (1898)   50

Korematsu v. United States (1944)   55

Brown v. Board of Education of Topeka (1954)   60

Cooper v. Aaron (1958)   65

Loving v. Virginia (1967)   71

Plyler v. Doe (1982)   76

Gratz v. Bollinger (2003)   85

Grutter v. Bollinger (2003)   93

Part III: FREEDOM OF SPEECH   113

Schenck v. United States (1919)   115

Brandenburg v. Ohio (1969)   118

Tinker v. Des Moines Independent Community School District (1969)   129

New York Times Company v. United States (1971)   136

Part IV: REPRODUCTIVE RIGHTS   141

Griswold v. Connecticut (1965)   143

Roe v. Wade (1973)   147

Planned Parenthood v. Casey (1992)   155

Dobbs v. Jackson Women's Health Organization (2022)   163

Part V: LGBTQ+ RIGHTS   183

Bowers v. Hardwick (1986)   185

Romer v. Evans (1996)   194

Lawrence v. Texas (2003)   198

Obergefell v. Hodges (2015)   202

Part VI: ELECTORAL PROCESSES   211

Baker v. Carr (1961)   213

Reynolds v. Sims (1964)   221

Shaw v. Reno (1993)   229

Citizens United v. Federal Election Commission (2010)   235

Acknowledgments   245

Unabridged Source Materials   247

Series Introduction

On November 9, 1989, the Berlin Wall fell. Two years later, in December 1991, the Soviet Union collapsed. These events, markers of the end of the Cold War, were seen by many as the final triumphant victory of democracy over authoritarianism and communism. Political scientist Francis Fukuyama famously declared the era to be the "end of history," suggesting that Western-style liberalism was the ultimate form of human ideology. There was a strong consensus—at least in the West—that liberal freedoms were necessary in any society.

But since then, that consensus has been shaken. In the twenty-first century, democracies have crumbled across the globe, with authoritarian leaders grabbing power and eroding traditional rights protections. Examples abound. Mexico and the Philippines embarked on extrajudicial drug wars; Nicolás Maduro's regime brought a state of near-famine to Venezuela; Poland's Law and Justice Party functionally turned parts of the media into its propaganda arm. In countless other countries, leaders have impinged on citizens' freedom. Even the United States—where liberal freedoms have often been taken for granted—has faced powerful movements and leaders who have disputed the legitimacy of the very rights that underpin our democracy.

Yet in the United States, calls to restrict rights have always run up against a powerful adversary, one that dates back to the country's founding: the Constitution of the United States. This Penguin Liberty series is designed to explore the Constitution's protections, illuminating how its text and values can help us as modern citizens to reflect on the meaning of liberty and understand how to defend it. With rights-based democracy under attack from all angles, it is crucial to engage in ongoing discussion about the meaning of liberty, its limits, and its role in the modern world.

Certainly, the ideal of liberty has been present in America since the dawn of the American Revolution, when Patrick Henry reportedly declared, "Give me liberty, or give me death!" In 1776, the Declaration of Independence proclaimed liberty an "unalienable Right"—along with "life" and the "pursuit of Happiness"—enshrining it as a central American aspiration.

These statements, however, are only a start in thinking about liberty. Mistakenly, they seem to suggest that liberty is absolute, never limited. But in this series, we will see that idea continually challenged. Various liberties sometimes conflict, and we must deliberate among them. Importantly, the liberty to be free from government intervention, or what the British philosopher Isaiah Berlin called "negative liberty," must sometimes be balanced against our liberty as a democratic people to govern in the general interest, an idea he called "positive liberty." Thus, the series will also emphasize the importance of liberty not only in terms of freedom from government intervention but also as self-government, the freedom of all of us collectively to decide on our own destinies.

Ratified in 1788, the Constitution was an attempt to codify the high ideal of liberty as self-government. Through intense debate at the Constitutional Convention, a document was forged that limited government power and gave people a say in how they were to be governed. Its goal was to "secure the Blessings of Liberty to ourselves and our Posterity." Still, many Americans were not convinced the Constitution went far enough in protecting their individual freedom from government coercion—what Berlin would call "negative liberty." Although the push for a Bill of Rights failed at the Constitutional Convention, the First Congress ratified one in 1791. These first ten amendments to the Constitution focused largely on securing individual liberties.

Just over 4,500 words long when originally passed, the U.S. Constitution is the shortest written governing charter of any major democracy. Its brevity belies its impact. Ours is the world's longest surviving written constitution. Some scholars estimate that, at one time, as many as 160 other nations based their constitution at least in part on the U.S. Constitution. The United Nations Universal Declaration of Human Rights from 1948 overlaps significantly with provisions of our Bill of Rights. Individual freedoms that our Constitution champions inspire peoples across the globe.

Of course, the original Constitution protected liberty for only a restricted few. As written in 1787, the Constitution did not explicitly outlaw racialized chattel slavery. Almost 700,000 Black people were enslaved in the United States at the time of its founding, a fact that the Constitution did nothing to change and tacitly allowed. Article I prohibited Congress from outlawing the international slave trade until 1808, and the three-fifths clause cemented Southern white political power by having enslaved people count toward political representation without allowing them to vote.

Not all the framers wanted the Constitution to be tainted by slavery. James Madison and Alexander Hamilton, for example, thought slavery morally wrong. But they were willing to compromise this conviction in order for Southern states to ratify the document they so cherished. Thus was born America's original sin, a legally sanctioned system of racial oppression that persisted formally until the Civil War. Only after an estimated more than 600,000 Americans gave their lives in that bloody conflict was the Constitution amended to outlaw slavery, guarantee "equal protection of the laws," and establish that race could deny no citizen access to the franchise.

Enslaved Americans were not the only ones left out of the original Constitution's promise of liberty. Women were guaranteed no formal rights under the Constitution, and they were deprived of equal political status until 1920, when suffragists finally succeeded in amending the Constitution to guarantee women the vote. In the Founding Era, the vote in many states was restricted mainly to white male property owners.

These significant failures are reasons to criticize the Constitution. But they should not lead anyone to discount it altogether. First, the Constitution has demonstrated a remarkable resilience and capacity for change. In each of the cases described above, the Constitution was later amended to attempt to rectify the wrong and expand citizens' rights. Second, and perhaps more important, the Constitution's deepest values have often inspired and strengthened the hand of those seeking justice. That's why Frederick Douglass, himself a former enslaved person, became an ardent supporter of the Constitution, even before the passage of the post–Civil War amendments that ended slavery and provided equal rights. In his Fourth of July oration in 1852, he praised the Constitution as a "glorious liberty document" but added a crucial caveat: it protected liberty only when it was "interpreted as it ought to be interpreted." Douglass believed that while many saw the Constitution as a pro-slavery document, its text and values supported broad protections for freedom and equality.

Douglass's point, though delivered more than 150 years ago, inspires this Penguin Liberty series. The Constitution is not a static document. Nor is it just a set of provisions on paper. The Constitution is a legal document containing specific rules, but it also gives voice to a broader public morality that transcends any one rule.

What exactly that public morality stands for has always been up for debate and interpretation. Today, after the passage of the post–Civil War amendments, the Constitution takes a clear stand against racial subordination. But there are still many other vital questions of liberty on which the Constitution offers guidance without dictating one definite answer. Through the processes of interpretation, amendment, and debate, the Constitution's guarantees of liberty have, over time, become more fully realized.

In these volumes, we will look to the Constitution's text and values, as well as to American history and some of its most important thinkers, to discover the best explanations of our constitutional ideals of liberty. Though imperfect, the Constitution can be the country's guiding light in dark times, illuminating a path to the recovery of liberty. My hope is that these volumes offer readers the chance to hear the strongest defenses of constitutional ideals, gaining new (or renewed) appreciation for values that have long sustained the nation.

No single fixed or perfectly clear meaning of the Constitution will emerge from this series. Constitutional statements of liberty are often brief, open to multiple interpretations. Competing values within the document raise difficult questions, such as how to balance freedom and equality, or privacy and security. I hope that as you learn from the important texts in these volumes, you undertake a critical examination of what liberty means to you—and how the Constitution should be interpreted to protect it. Though the popular understanding may be that the Supreme Court is the final arbiter of the Constitution, constitutional liberty is best protected when not just every branch of government but also every citizen is engaged in constitutional interpretation. Questions of liberty affect both our daily lives and our country's values, from what we can say to whom we can marry, how society views us to how we determine our leaders. It is Americans' great privilege that we live under a Constitution that both protects our liberty and allows us to debate what that liberty should be.

The central features of constitutional liberty are freedom and equality, values that are often in tension. One of the Constitution's most important declarations of freedom comes in the First Amendment, which provides that "Congress shall make no law respecting an establishment of religion, or prohibiting the free exercise thereof; or abridging the freedom of speech, or of the press; or the right of the people peaceably to assemble, and to petition the Government for a redress of grievances." And one of its most important declarations of equality comes in the Fourteenth Amendment, which reads in part, "no State shall . . . deny to any person within its jurisdiction the equal protection of the laws." These Penguin Liberty volumes look in depth at these conceptions of liberty while also exploring what mechanisms the Constitution has to protect its guarantees of liberty.

Freedom of speech provides a good place to begin to explore the Constitution's idea of liberty. It is a value that enables both the protection of liberty and the right of citizens to debate its meaning. Textually, the constitutional guarantee that Congress cannot limit free speech might read as though it is absolute. Yet for much of U.S. history, free speech protections were minimal. In 1798, President John Adams signed the

Sedition Act, essentially making it a crime to criticize the president or the U.S. government. During the Civil War, President Abraham Lincoln had some dissidents and newspapers silenced. In 1919, a moment came that seemed to protect free speech, when Justice Oliver Wendell Holmes wrote in *Schenck v. United States* that speech could be limited only when it posed a "clear and present danger." But, in fact, this ruling did little to protect free speech, as the Court repeatedly interpreted danger so broadly that minority viewpoints, especially leftist viewpoints, were often punishable by imprisonment.

Today, however, U.S. free speech protections are the most expansive in the world. All viewpoints are allowed to be expressed, except for direct threats and incitements to violence. Even many forms of hate speech and opinions attacking democracy itself—types of speech that would be illegal in other countries—are generally permitted here, in the name of free expression. The Court's governing standard is annunciated in *Brandenburg v. Ohio*, which protects vast amounts of speech as long as that speech does not incite "imminent lawless action." How did we get from the Sedition Act to here?

Two thinkers have played an outsize role: John Stuart Mill and Alexander Meiklejohn. Mill's 1859 classic, *On Liberty,* is an ode to the idea that both liberty and truth will thrive in an open exchange of ideas, where all opinions are allowed to be challenged. In this "marketplace of ideas," as Mill's idea has often come to be called, the truth stays vibrant instead of decaying or descending into dogma. Mill's idea explains the virtue of free speech and the importance of a book series about liberty: challenging accepted ideas about what liberty is helps bring the best ideas to light. Meiklejohn's theory focuses more on the connection between free speech and democracy. To him, the value of free speech is as much for the listeners as it is for the speakers. In a democracy, only when citizens hear all ideas can they come to informed conclusions about how society should be governed. And only informed citizens can fully exercise other democratic rights besides speech, like the right to vote. Meiklejohn's insistence that democratic citizens need a broad exposure to ideas of liberty inspires this series.

Freedom of religion is another central constitutional value that allows citizens the liberty to be who they are and believe what they wish. It is enshrined in the First Amendment, where the Establishment Clause prevents government endorsement of a religion and the Free Exercise Clause gives citizens the freedom to practice their religion. Though these two religion clauses are widely embraced now, they were radically new at the time of the nation's founding. Among the first European settlers in America were the Puritans, members of a group of English Protestants who were persecuted for their religion in their native Britain. But colonial America did not immediately and totally embrace religious toleration. The Church of England still held great sway in the South during the colonial era, and many states had official religions—even after the Constitution forbade a national religion. At the time the Constitution was ratified, secular government was a rarity.

But religious tolerance was eventually enshrined in the U.S. Constitution, thanks in large part to the influence of two thinkers. British philosopher John Locke opposed systems of theocracy. He saw how government-imposed religious beliefs stifled the freedom of minority believers and imposed religious dogma on unwilling societies. In the United States, James Madison built on Locke's ideas when he drafted the First Amendment. The Free Exercise Clause protected the personal freedom to worship, acknowledging the importance of religious practice among Americans. But on Madison's understanding, the Establishment Clause ensured against theocratic imposition of religion by government. Doing so respected the equality of citizens by refusing to allow the government to favor some people's religious beliefs over others'.

A more explicit defense of equality comes from the Equal Protection Clause of the Fourteenth Amendment. But as our volume on the Supreme Court shows, the Constitution has not always been interpreted to promote equality. Before the Civil War, African Americans had few, if any, formal rights. Millions of African American people were enslaved, and so-called congressional compromises maintained racial subordination long after the importation of slaves was banned in 1808. A burgeoning abolitionist movement gained moral momentum in the North, though the institution of slavery persisted. Liberty was a myth for enslaved people, who were unable to move freely, form organizations, earn wages, or participate in politics.

Still, the Supreme Court, the supposed protector of liberty, for decades failed to guarantee it for African Americans. And in its most notorious ruling it revealed the deep-seated prejudices that had helped to perpetuate slavery. Chief Justice Roger Taney wrote in the 1857 decision in *Dred Scott v. Sandford* that African Americans were not citizens of the United States and "had no rights which the white man was bound to respect." Taney's words were one spark for the Civil War, which, once won by the Union, led to the passage of the Thirteenth, Fourteenth, and Fifteenth Amendments. By ending slavery, granting citizenship and mandating equal legal protection, and outlawing racial discrimination in voting, these Reconstruction Amendments sought to reverse Taney's heinous opinion and provide a platform for advancing real equality.

History unfortunately shows us, however, that legal equality did not translate into real equality for African Americans. Soon after Reconstruction, the Court eviscerated the

Fourteenth Amendment's scope, then ruled in 1896 in *Plessy v. Ferguson* that racial segregation was constitutional if the separate facilities were deemed equal. This paved the way for the legally sanctioned institution of Jim Crow segregation, which relegated African Americans to second-class citizenship, denying them meaningful social, legal, and political equality. Finally, facing immense pressure from civil rights advocates including W. E. B. Du Bois and A. Philip Randolph, as well as the powerful legal reasoning of NAACP lawyer Thurgood Marshall, the Court gave the Equal Protection Clause teeth, culminating in the landmark 1954 *Brown v. Board of Education* decision, which declared that separate is "inherently unequal." Even after that newfound defense of constitutional equality, however, racial inequality has persisted, with the Court and country debating the meaning of liberty and equal protection in issues as varied as affirmative action and racial gerrymandering.

While the Fourteenth Amendment was originally passed with a specific intention to end racial discrimination, its language is general: "No State shall . . . deny to any person within its jurisdiction the equal protection of the laws." Over time, that generality has allowed civil rights advocates to expand the meaning of equality to include other groups facing discrimination. One significant example is the fight for gender equality.

Women had been left out of the Constitution; masculine pronouns pepper the original document, and women are not mentioned. In an 1807 letter to Albert Gallatin, Thomas Jefferson—the person who had penned the Declaration of Independence—wrote that "the appointment of a woman to office is an innovation for which the public is not prepared, nor am I." Liberty was a myth for many women, who were supposed to do little outside the home, had limited rights to property, were often made to be financially dependent on their husbands, and faced immense barriers to political participation.

Nevertheless, women refused to be shut out of politics. Many were influential in the burgeoning temperance and abolition movements of the nineteenth century. In 1848, Elizabeth Cady Stanton wrote the Declaration of Sentiments, amending the Declaration of Independence to include women. Still, suffragists were left out when the Fifteenth Amendment banned voting discrimination based on race—but not on gender. Only after Alice Paul and others led massive protests would the freedom to vote be constitutionally guaranteed for women through the Nineteenth Amendment.

Voting secured one key democratic liberty, but women were still denied the full protection of legal equality. They faced discrimination in the workplace, laws based on sexist stereotypes, and a lack of reproductive autonomy. That's where our volume on Supreme Court Justice Ruth Bader Ginsburg begins. Now a feminist icon from her opinions on the Court, Justice Ginsburg earlier served as a litigator with the ACLU, leading their Women's Rights Project, where she helped to convince the Court to consider gender as a protected class under the Fourteenth Amendment. As a justice, she continued her pioneering work to deliver real gender equality, knowing that women would never enjoy the full scope of constitutional liberty unless they held the same legal status as men.

Ginsburg's work underscores how the meaning of constitutional liberty has expanded over time. While the Declaration of Independence did explicitly reference equality, the Bill of Rights did not. Then, with the Reconstruction Amendments, especially the Equal Protection Clause, the Constitution was imbued with a new commitment to equality. Now the document affirmed that democratic societies must protect both negative liberties for citizens to act freely and positive liberties for all to be treated as equal democratic citizens. Never has this tension between freedom and equality been perfectly resolved, but the story of our Constitution is that it has often inspired progress toward realizing liberty for more Americans.

Progress has been possible not just because of an abstract constitutional commitment to liberty, but also due to formal mechanisms that help us to guarantee it. Impeachment is the Constitution's most famous—and most explosive—way to do so. With the abuses of monarchy in mind, the framers needed a way to thwart tyranny and limit concentrated power. Borrowing in language and spirit from the British, who created a system of impeachment to check the power of the king, they wrote this clause into the Constitution: "The President . . . shall be removed from Office on Impeachment for, and Conviction of, Treason, Bribery, or other high Crimes and Misdemeanors."

Early drafts suggested grounds for impeachment should be just "treason or bribery." But George Mason and other delegates objected, wanting impeachable offenses to include broader abuses of power, not just criminal actions. Though Mason's original suggestion of "maladministration" was rejected, the ultimate language of "high Crimes and Misdemeanors" made it possible to pursue impeachment against leaders who threatened the Constitution's deeper values. Impeachment would stand as the ultimate check on officials who have overstepped their constitutional authority.

The House has formally impeached twenty officials throughout American history, and many more have faced some kind of impeachment inquiry. Most of those accused have been federal judges. Just five impeachment proceedings have reached the presidency, the highest echelon of American government. Andrew Johnson and Bill Clinton were each formally impeached once and Donald Trump was formally impeached twice, though none of these presidents were convicted and removed from office. Richard Nixon resigned after the House Judiciary Committee voted to impeach, before the full House vote could take place. Most of these impeachment proceedings had a background context in which a president was thought to have violated fundamental constitutional liberties—even if that violation was not always the primary component of the impeachment hearings themselves.

For Johnson, although his impeachment focused on the Tenure of Office Act, an underlying issue was his violation of the liberty of newly freed African Americans to live in society as equals. For Nixon, the impeachment inquiry focused on the Watergate break-in and cover-up, which threatened the liberty of voters to have fair elections and to hold their presidents criminally accountable. For Clinton, who was accused of perjury and obstruction of justice related to a sexual affair with a White House intern, critics argued that his flouting of criminal laws threatened the standard of equal justice under law—a standard necessary for democratic self-government. For Trump, the impeachment articles in his first trial accused him of soliciting foreign interference as an abuse of power—threatening the liberty of voters to have fair elections; and his second impeachment trial accused him of inciting an insurrection to prevent the peaceful transfer of power between administrations, threatening that previously uninterrupted hallmark of American democracy. Often, legalistic questions of criminal wrongdoing dominated these impeachment discussions, but concerns about violations of constitutional liberty were frequently present in the background.

While impeachment is an important remedy for presidential abuse of liberty, liberty lives best when it is respected before crises arise. To do so requires that liberty not be relegated to an idea just for the purview of courts; rather, citizens and officials should engage in discussions about the meaning of liberty, reaffirming its centrality in everyday life.

By few people are those discussions better modeled than by the example of the now musically famous Alexander Hamilton, a founding father and the nation's first secretary of the treasury. Hamilton was a prolific writer, and in our volumes we'll see him square off against other founders in debates on many major challenges facing the early republic. Against Samuel Seabury, Hamilton rejected the British colonial system and said liberty must come through independence. Against Thomas Jefferson (in an argument now immortalized as a Broadway rap battle), Hamilton advocated for a national bank, believing that a modern, industrial economy was needed to grow the nation. Against James Madison, he pushed for stronger foreign policy powers for the president.

The specifics of Hamilton's debates matter. His ideas shaped American notions of government power, from self-determination to economic growth to international engagement. He was instrumental in ratifying the very Constitution that still protects our liberties today. But just as important as *what* he argued for was *how* he argued for it. Hamilton thought deeply about what liberty meant to him, and he engaged in thoughtful, reasoned discussions with people he disagreed with. He cared both for his own freedoms and for the country's welfare at large.

My goal is for readers of these Penguin Liberty volumes to emulate Hamilton's passion for defending his ideas—even, or especially, if they disagree with him on what liberty means. Everyday citizens are the most important readers of this series—and the most important Americans in the struggle to protect and expand constitutional liberty. Without pressure from the citizenry to uphold constitutional ideals, elected leaders can too easily scrap them. Without citizens vigorously examining the meaning of liberty, its power could be lost. Left untended, the flames of liberty could quietly burn out.

The writings in these Penguin Liberty volumes are intended to give citizens the tools to contest and explore the meaning of liberty so it may be kept alive. None of the selections are simple enough to be summed up in tweets or dismissed with quick insults. They are reasoned, thoughtful attempts to defend constitutional ideals of liberty—or warnings about what can happen when those liberties are disregarded. The Constitution's guarantees of liberty have always been aspirations, not realized accomplishments. Yet if these volumes and other constitutional writings inspire us to bring discussions to dinner tables, classrooms, and workplaces across the country, they will be contributing to making those high ideals more real.

COREY BRETTSCHNEIDER

Introduction

Why read the classic cases? The purpose of the Penguin Liberty series is to encourage citizens to think for themselves about the meaning of freedom under our Constitution. So why devote a volume to classic cases of the Supreme Court, given that they are often thought to be written by lawyers and judges for lawyers and judges? Indeed, legal training for law students entails reading judicial decisions as a means of preparing to enter the profession.

In this volume, however, I present Supreme Court cases not as fodder for future lawyers but as materials to be read, studied, and engaged with by citizens concerned with playing their part in our democracy. Each case plays a crucial role in a much-needed national conversation about the rights and liberties we owe to one another as members of the American polity. And they are edited to make them accessible to citizen readers, who cannot rely on legal professionals to interpret their rights for them.

The opinions here are not meant as ready-made explanations of our liberties. Instead, they are documents to stimulate reflection. Supreme Court practice, as opposed to legislative decision making, lends itself particularly well to that endeavor. This is because the Supreme Court does not simply vote like a legislature. It, by custom, explains its reasoning in opinions. Majority opinions therefore make transparent why the Court has or has not protected free speech or religious liberty in a particular case. And its reasoning stands as something to be reflected on by citizen readers, criticized, or affirmed.

And while majority opinions allow citizens to reflect on the past decisions of the Court, the opinions by dissenting justices also play a crucial role in stimulating discussion about the meaning of the Constitution. These dissents show that the question of what liberties our Constitution protects is itself contested within the Court. The dissents are often sharp disagreements with majority decisions about the meaning of our Constitution. The willingness of justices to dissent should also be an invitation for readers to develop their own ideas of constitutional meaning even when they run contrary to the majority opinions. My hope is that in reading these cases and prominent dissents, citizens will be willing, when they find something wrong, to themselves dissent and speak out about the Court's past wrongdoing. That willingness to be an active interpreter of the Constitution is fundamental to what I called in the series introduction, following Isaiah Berlin, "positive liberty": a willingness of citizens to actively engage themselves in demanding their liberties as participants in self-government, not being mere passive subjects of our institutions.

I have emphasized the importance of citizen interpretation of the Constitution. But the Supreme Court has, not surprisingly, emphasized the centrality of its own interpretation, sometimes indicating that it has the final say about the meaning of the document and of our liberties. For instance, the reasoning of one classic case, *Marbury v. Madison* (1803), emphasizes that since law is interpreted exclusively by judges, only judges should interpret the Constitution because it is the supreme law. That view is bolstered by the structure of

Article III, which might be thought to grant exclusive power to judges on matters of law, even though it does not explicitly do so. Such a rigid understanding would leave little room for the kind of citizen interpretation I am urging. But is it correct?

The inconsistency of the Court's own judgments across its history reveals that it is at least partly flawed. While courts have an established power to review legislation, a power that is often justified by the logic of *Marbury*, repeatedly the Court has made decisions that it has come to view not just as wrong, but evil. Included here in the canon of classic cases like *Brown v. Board of Education of Topeka* (1954) are a number of flawed and even evil decisions. It will be clear upon reading them that to say that a case is "classic" or seminal does not imply that it is rightly decided. Far from it. A classic case is simply one that is is important in our history. Therefore, it is urgent that citizens examine any such case and its logic with skepticism and a willingness to dissent.

With an eye to encouraging skepticism that the Supreme Court has the final say about the meaning of the Constitution, the classic cases included here often are those that constitute an embarrassing legacy of American history. They are included to motivate independence of thought by citizen readers and to highlight the importance of not simply deferring to the Supreme Court. For examples of the Court's willingness to undermine liberty rather than protect it, I most prominently include *Dred Scott v. Sandford* (1857), which tragically denied legal personhood to Black people under the Constitution before the Civil War. I also include *Korematsu v. United States* (1944), which upheld the forced internment of Japanese Americans during World War II based on the government's false and frivolous argument that there were significant numbers of disloyal Japanese Americans in the population. Readers should be appalled by these cases; they stand as a testament to why the Supreme Court should never have a monopoly on the correct understanding of the Constitution. Simply put, the Supreme Court often fails deeply in its role. But far from inviting pessimism, these opinions should empower readers to think for themselves and not bow down to any official interpretation.

Of these wrongly decided opinions that should stir outrage and thought among readers, the majority opinion in *Plessy v. Ferguson* (1896) stands out for its complicity in the nineteenth- and early twentieth-century practice of racial subordination widely known as "segregation." In that case, the Supreme Court mangled the words "equal protection," written into the Constitution to help ensure Black equality under law after the Civil War, to allow for a form of American apartheid—a system of racial subordination based on race. Falsely, *Plessy* claimed that the vast system of apartheid was "separate but equal."

But as morally and legally flawed as the *Plessy* opinion was, it also contained the seeds of hope to which readers may look in thinking about the meaning of equality in a free society. The *Plessy* opinion contained a dissent by Justice Harlan that would eventually be vindicated by the Court in the *Brown* decision and subsequent holdings. To be sure, in his dissent, Harlan perpetuated some of the white supremacist ideas present in the majority's opinion, but he still argued that the misguided and false idea of "separate but equal" undermined the true idea of equal protection. In Harlan's view, equal protection was meant to stop a system of subordination based on race, a system inherited from American slavery.

The road to overturning *Plessy* was long and hard fought, largely driven by the NAACP's citizen activism and its legal defense fund. By 1954, the organization had finally convinced the Court to undo *Plessy*'s holding of "separate but equal" in

Brown v. Board of Education. Brown is rightly lauded as a seminal case in American history and a long overdue vindication of Harlan's dissent.

But the job of citizens in thinking for themselves about the meaning of "equal protection" was far from finished after the Court's reversal of *Plessy* in *Brown*. Debate continues today about what it means for "separate" to be "inherently unequal." As two cases excerpted here about race-conscious affirmative action programs at the University of Michigan undergraduate and law school show, some justices have argued that Harlan's idea of subordination requires a "colorblind" Constitution, meaning that government attempts to desegregate our society through affirmative action were unconstitutional. Increasingly that interpretation of Harlan has taken hold. In particular, Justice Clarence Thomas has taken up this argument in dissents in affirmative action cases, arguing that affirmative action violates the Constitution's colorblindness principle and harms racial minorities more than it benefits them. Significantly, that interpretation was rejected by the NAACP, whose legal defense fund litigated *Brown v. Board of Education* but did not intend to oppose affirmative action. Citizen readers of the Constitution are asked to think for themselves about the meaning of the phrase "equal protection" by reading majority and dissenting opinions from these relatively recent cases about affirmative action at the University of Michigan.

Citizen interpretation of the Constitution is a crucial check on all branches of the government, and the next part of the volume focuses on the fundamental First Amendment right so essential to cultivating strong citizen interpreters: free speech. This right is the very linchpin of democracy. However, while the Court has often lauded free speech, it has not always protected it. For instance, in 1919's *Schenk v.*

United States, the Court severely restricted speech, citing security concerns. It later sought to correct this overreach in cases like *Brandenberg v. Ohio*. Familiarizing themselves with these classic free speech cases will help citizen interpreters to continue defending this fundamental democratic right.

One of the most contentious areas in modern American life concerns the question of whether abortion should be legal. This question is one of several related to reproductive rights that are explored through cases in the next part of the volume. In 2022, the Supreme Court made a monumental decision, included in this volume, that reversed *Roe v. Wade* (1973), the case that had established the right to abortion. As Justice Alito, writing for a majority of the Court put it, "*Roe* was egregiously wrong from the start." Alito argued that there was no right to abortion written into the Constitution's text and that an examination of history shows this not to be a right grounded in the American legal tradition. The *Dobbs v. Jackson Women's Health Organization* (2022) decision marked a seismic shift in the Court's approach to reproductive freedom and triggered a national outcry that the Court was acting politically by reversing long-standing precedent. To defend abortion rights, however, readers need to do more than simply cite precedent. After all, *Brown v. Board of Education* reversed a long-standing precedent too, but that case is rightly lauded, not decried.

How might a defender of abortion rights critically confront the *Dobbs v. Jackson Women's Health Organization* decision? One option is to turn for inspiration to arguments found in *Griswold v. Connecticut* (1965), which established the Constitutional right to birth control, included as the first case in our section on reproductive freedom. That case provided an important basis for the decision in *Roe*. *Dobbs* claimed that its overturning of *Roe* was consistent with respect to the principles espoused in *Griswold*. But is it? *Griswold* presented a theory of liberty beyond what is explicitly mentioned in the Constitution. In defending a broad right of "privacy," the *Griswold* opinion instead argued for an understanding of the Constitution based in broad principles espoused in the Bill of Rights. *Griswold* itself concerned the right of married couples to use contraception. Justice Douglass's opinion in that case argued that while that specific right was not mentioned by the framers in the text of the Constitution, it is implicit in the document's "penumbras," in other words, a right to autonomous decisions is a theme throughout the Constitution. That logic about contraception is deeply at odds with Alito's attack on *Roe* in *Dobbs* and an important resource for those who wish to criticize it.

Another question raised by Alito's opinion in *Dobbs* is about the Court's protection of LGBTQ+ rights. As our section on LGBTQ+ rights shows readers, this is an area of increasingly expansive constitutional protection. Although originally disparaging of the idea that the constitutional right to privacy included a right of sexual intimacy for gay couples free of government intervention, the Court came to change its mind. In *Lawrence v. Texas* (2003), the Court expanded the right to privacy to include a right to liberty in individual decisions concerning one's physical relationships. And in its seminal *Obergefell v. Hodges* (2015) decision, the Court drew on *Lawrence* to extend the previously recognized fundamental right to marriage to same-sex couples, enabling marriage equality. Alito in *Dobbs* claims that this decision about abortion does not unmoor the decisions in *Lawrence* and *Obergefell*, just as it does not undo the decision in *Griswold*. But readers wishing to defend those rights should be skeptical. If *Dobbs* proposes to read the Constitution by looking only for explicit protections or those protected historically at the founding, gay rights seem on such a reading to be on a shaky foundation. A critical citizen reader then must read *Dobbs* alongside the classic cases in the LGBTQ+ section, asking whether these precedents too are now under threat. And how could a citizen reader defend LGBTQ+ rights against the potential assault suggested by the *Dobbs* decision? Here *Griswold* might again be a helpful resource. Liberty is protected in the Constitution as a broad theme, not through specific provisions. And a reading to the contrary, as suggested by *Dobbs*, would be to strip the various provisions of their meaning, just as breaking a poem down only to its words would fail to see its broader point. LGBTQ+ rights are not an outlier of constitutional liberty. They are based in the fundamental idea that the Constitution protects individual liberty from government overreach.

The final part of the volume focuses on cases that concern a right central to any democracy: the right to vote. This part highlights debates about the Court's role in shaping legislative districts and in protecting the right of corporations to engage in campaign speech. At a time when our system of national elections is under assault by conspiracy theorists and others, the debate over the role of the Court in protecting democracy could not be more fundamental. However, delving into these cases will not reveal a ready-made answer but a series of debates between the justices over whether the Court should be the bulwark of democracy.

This volume gives citizens the tools to analyze the most fundamental questions of liberty in our society today. The cases should inspire at times and enrage at others. Read them with a skeptical eye. Think for yourself about them. In doing so, you will be exercising the primary freedom in a democracy: to think for yourself.

COREY BRETTSCHNEIDER

A Note on the Text

All the works in this volume are excerpted from full Supreme Court opinions. Spelling and punctuation are kept as in the original. Footnotes have been eliminated from the text without marking. All works can be found in the Unabridged Source Materials section at the end of this book.

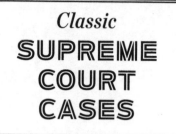

Classic

SUPREME COURT CASES

Part I

ORIGINS OF
JUDICIAL REVIEW

These two cases from early in the American republic establish the Supreme Court's power of judicial review, the power to decide if laws and actions by the government conflict with the United States Constitution or other laws. This power is nowhere explicitly outlined in the Constitution, so the justices came up with reasons that were based on the nature of lawmaking and judging to explain why they had such a power. As you read the cases, think about whether this power is consistent with the basic principles of democracy. And if the Supreme Court should have this power, is it compatible with a role for citizens also opining on the meaning of our liberties under the Constitution?

Calder v. Bull
(1798)

> *This case clarified the Constitution's prohibition of* ex
> post facto *laws, or laws that retroactively make an act
> illegal after it has been legally committed. In this case,
> the Supreme Court ruled that the Constitution's* ex post
> facto *clause applied to certain criminal laws, but not
> civil ones.*

The Legislature of Connecticut, on the 2d Thursday of May,
1795, passed a resolution or law which . . . set aside a decree
of the Court of Probate for Harford on 21 March 1793,
which decree disapproved of the will of Normand Morrison
(the grandson) made 21 August, 1779, and refused to record
the said will, and granted a new hearing by the said court of
probate with liberty of appeal therefrom in six months. A
new hearing was had in virtue of this resolution or law
before the said court of probate, which, on 27 July, 1795, approved the said will and ordered it to be recorded. At August,
1795, appeal was then had to the Superior Court at Hartford,
which, at February term, 1796, affirmed the decree of the
court of probate. Appeal was had to the Supreme Court of
Errors of Connecticut, which, in June, 1796, adjudged that

there were no errors. More than 18 months elapsed from the decree of the court of probate (on 1 March, 1793) and thereby Caleb Bull and wife were barred of all right of appeal by a statute of Connecticut. There was no law of that state whereby a new hearing or trial before the said court of probate might be obtained. Calder and wife claim the premises in question, in right of his wife as heiress of N. Morrison, physician; Bull and wife claim under the will of N. Morrison, the grandson.

The counsel for the plaintiffs in error contend that the said resolution or law of the Legislature of Connecticut granting a new hearing in the above case is an *ex post facto* law, prohibited by the Constitution of the United States; that any law of the federal government or of any of the state governments contrary to the Constitution of the United States is void, and that this Court possesses the power to declare such law void.

It appears to me a self-evident proposition that the several state legislatures retain all the powers of legislation delegated to them by the state constitutions which are not expressly taken away by the Constitution of the United States. The establishing of courts of justice, the appointment of judges, and the making regulations for the administration of justice within each state according to its laws on all subjects not entrusted to the federal government appears to me to be the peculiar and exclusive province and duty of the state legislatures. All the powers delegated by the people of the United States to the federal government are defined, and no constructive powers can be exercised by it, and all the powers that remain in the state governments are indefinite except only in the Constitution of Massachusetts.

The effect of the resolution or law of Connecticut above stated is to revise a decision of one of its inferior courts, called the Court of Probate for Hartford, and to direct a new hearing of the case by the same court of probate, that passed the decree against the will of Normand Morrison. By the existing law of Connecticut, a right to recover certain property had vested in Calder and wife (the appellants) in consequence of a decision of a court of justice, but, in virtue of a subsequent resolution or law and the new hearing thereof and the decision in consequence, this right to recover certain property was divested, and the right to the property declared to be in Bull and wife, the appellees. The sole inquiry is whether this resolution or law of Connecticut, having such operation, is an *ex post facto* law within the prohibition of the federal Constitution.

Whether the legislature of any of the states can revise and correct by law a decision of any of its courts of justice, although not prohibited by the constitution of the state, is a question of very great importance, and not necessary now to be determined, because the resolution or law in question does not go so far. . . . The nature and ends of legislative power will limit the exercise of it. This fundamental principle flows from the very nature of our free republican governments that no man should be compelled to do what the laws do not require nor to refrain from acts which the laws permit. There are acts which the federal or state legislature cannot do without exceeding their authority. . . . An act of the legislature (for I cannot call it a law) contrary to the great first principles of the social compact cannot be considered a rightful exercise of legislative authority. The obligation of a law in governments established on express compact and on republican principles must be determined by the nature of the power on which it is founded.

A few instances will suffice to explain what I mean. A law that punished a citizen for an innocent action, or in other words for an act which when done was in violation of no existing law; a law that destroys or impairs the lawful private contracts of citizens; a law that makes a man a judge in his own cause, or a law that takes property from A. and gives it to B. It is against all reason and justice for a people to entrust a legislature with such powers, and therefore it cannot be presumed that it has done it. The genius, the nature, and the spirit of our state governments amount to a prohibition of such acts of legislation, and the general principles of law and reason forbid them. The legislature may enjoin, permit, forbid, and punish; it may declare new crimes and establish rules of conduct for all its citizens in future cases; it may command what is right and prohibit what is wrong, but it cannot change innocence into guilt or punish innocence as a crime or violate the right of an antecedent lawful private contract or the right of private property. To maintain that our federal or state legislature possesses such powers if it had not been expressly restrained would, in my opinion, be a political heresy altogether inadmissible in our free republican governments.

All the restrictions contained in the Constitution of the United States on the power of the state legislatures were provided in favor of the authority of the federal government. The prohibition against its making any *ex post facto* laws was introduced for greater caution, and very probably arose from the knowledge that the Parliament of Great Britain claimed and exercised a power to pass such laws under the denomination of bills of attainder or bills of pains and penalties, the first inflicting capital and the other less punishment. These acts were legislative judgments and an exercise of judicial power. . . . The ground for the exercise of such legislative power was this, that the safety of the kingdom depended on the death or other punishment of the offender, as if traitors, when discovered, could be so formidable or the government so insecure! With very few exceptions, the advocates of such laws were stimulated by ambition or personal resentment and vindictive malice. To prevent such and similar, acts of violence and injustice, I believe, the federal and state legislatures were prohibited from passing any bill of attainder or any *ex post facto* law.

The Constitution of the United States, Article I, section 9, prohibits the Legislature of the United States from passing any *ex post facto* law, and in section 10 lays several restrictions on the authority of the legislatures of the several states, and among them "that no state shall pass any *ex post facto* law." . . .

I shall endeavor to show what law is to be considered an *ex post facto* law within the words and meaning of the prohibition in the federal Constitution. The prohibition "that no state shall pass any *ex post facto* law" necessarily requires some explanation, for naked and without explanation it is unintelligible and means nothing. Literally, it is only that a law shall not be passed concerning and after the fact or thing done or action committed. I would ask, what fact, of what nature, or kind, and by whom done? That Charles I, King of England, was beheaded, that Oliver Cromwell was Protector of England, that Louis XVI, late King of France, was guillotined, are all facts that have happened, but it would be nonsense to suppose that the states were prohibited from making any law after either of these events and with reference thereto. The prohibition in the letter is not to pass any law concerning and after the fact, but the plain and obvious meaning and intention of the prohibition is this—that the legislatures of the several states shall not pass laws after a fact done by a subject or citizen which shall have relation to such fact and shall punish him for having done it. The prohibition, considered in this light, is an additional bulwark in favor of the personal security of the subject, to protect his person from punishment by legislative acts having a retrospective operation. . . .

I will state what laws I consider *ex post facto* laws within the words and the intent of the prohibition. 1st. Every law that makes an action done before the passing of the law and which was innocent when done, criminal and punishes such action. 2d. Every law that aggravates a crime, or makes it greater than it was when committed. 3rd. Every law that changes the punishment, and inflicts a greater punishment than the law annexed to the crime, when committed. 4th. Every law that alters the legal rules of evidence and receives less or different testimony than the law required at the time of the commission of the offense in order to convict the offender.

All these and similar laws are manifestly unjust and oppressive. In my opinion, the true distinction is between *ex post facto* laws and retrospective laws. Every *ex post facto* law must necessarily be retrospective, but every retrospective law is not an *ex post facto* law. The former only are prohibited. . . . Every law that is to have an operation before the making thereof, as to commence at an antecedent time or to save time from the statute of limitations or to excuse acts which were unlawful, and before committed, and the like, is retrospective. But such laws may be proper or necessary, as the case may be. There is a great and apparent difference between making an unlawful act lawful and the making an innocent action criminal and punishing it as a crime. The expressions "*ex post facto* laws" are technical; they had been in use long before the Revolution, and had acquired an appropriate meaning, by legislators, lawyers, and authors. . . .

In the present case there is no fact done by Bull and wife plaintiffs in error, that is in any manner affected by the law or resolution of Connecticut. It does not concern or relate to any act done by them. The decree of the Court of Probate of Hartford (on 21 March) in consequence of which Calder and wife claim a right to the property in question was given before the said law or resolution, . . . in consequence of the law allowing a hearing and the decision in favor of the will, they have lost what they would have been entitled to if the law or resolution, and the decision in consequence thereof, had not been made. The decree of the court of probate is the only fact on which the law or resolution operates. In my judgment, the case of the plaintiffs in error is not within the letter of the prohibition, and for the reasons assigned I am clearly of opinion that it is not within the intention of the prohibition, and if within the intention but out of the letter, I should not, therefore, consider myself justified to continue it within the prohibition, and therefore that the whole was void. . . .

I am of opinion that the decree of the Supreme Court of Errors of Connecticut be affirmed with costs.

Marbury v. Madison
(1803)

> *This landmark case established the precedent of judicial review, which refers to the Supreme Court's power to declare a law or other government action unconstitutional or invalid.*

Mr. Chief Justice MARSHALL delivered the opinion of the Court.

At the last term, on the affidavits then read and filed with the clerk, a rule was granted in this case requiring the Secretary of State to show cause why a mandamus should not issue directing him to deliver to William Marbury his commission as a justice of the peace for the county of Washington, in the District of Columbia.

No cause has been shown, and the present motion is for a mandamus. The peculiar delicacy of this case . . . require[s] a complete exposition of the principles on which the opinion to be given by the Court is founded. . . .

In the order in which the Court has viewed this subject, the following questions have been considered and decided.

1. Has the applicant a right to the commission he demands?

2. If he has a right, and that right has been violated, do the laws of his country afford him a remedy?

3. If they do afford him a remedy, is it a mandamus issuing from this court?

The first object of inquiry is:

1. Has the applicant a right to the commission he demands?

His right originates in an act of Congress passed in February, 1801, concerning the District of Columbia.

After dividing the district into two counties, the eleventh section of this law enacts, "that there shall be appointed in and for each of the said counties such number of discreet persons to be justices of the peace as the President of the United States shall, from time to time, think expedient, to continue in office for five years."

It appears from the affidavits that, in compliance with this law, a commission for William Marbury as a justice of peace for the County of Washington was signed by John Adams, then President of the United States, after which the seal of the United States was affixed to it, but the commission has never reached the person for whom it was made out.

In order to determine whether he is entitled to this commission, it becomes necessary to inquire whether he has been appointed to the office. . . .

The acts of appointing to office and commissioning the person appointed can scarcely be considered as one and the same, since the power to perform them is given in two separate and distinct sections of the Constitution. . . .

This is an appointment made by the President, by and with the advice and consent of the Senate, and is evidenced by no act but the commission itself. In such a case, therefore, the commission and the appointment seem inseparable, it being almost impossible to show an appointment otherwise than by proving the existence of a commission; still, the commission is not necessarily the appointment; though conclusive evidence of it.

But at what stage does it amount to this conclusive evidence?

The answer to this question seems an obvious one. The appointment, being the sole act of the President, must be completely evidenced when it is shown that he has done everything to be performed by him.

Should the commission, instead of being evidence of an appointment, even be considered as constituting the appointment itself, still it would be made when the last act to be done by the President was performed, or, at furthest, when the commission was complete.

The last act to be done by the President is the signature of the commission. . . . His judgment, on the advice and consent of the Senate concurring with his nomination, has been made, and the officer is appointed. . . .

The signature is a warrant for affixing the great seal to the commission, and the great seal is only to be affixed to an instrument which is complete. It attests, by an act supposed to be of public notoriety, the verity of the Presidential signature.

It is never to be affixed till the commission is signed, because the signature, which gives force and effect to the commission, is conclusive evidence that the appointment is made. . . .

It is therefore decidedly the opinion of the Court that, when a commission has been signed by the President, the appointment is made, and that the commission is complete when the seal of the United States has been affixed to it by the Secretary of State. . . .

Mr. Marbury, then, since his commission was signed by the President and sealed by the Secretary of State, was appointed, and as the law creating the office gave the officer a right to hold for five years independent of the Executive, the appointment was not revocable, but vested in the officer legal rights which are protected by the laws of his country.

To withhold the commission, therefore, is an act deemed by the Court not warranted by law, but violative of a vested legal right.

This brings us to the second inquiry, which is:

2. If he has a right, and that right has been violated, do the laws of his country afford him a remedy?

The very essence of civil liberty certainly consists in the right of every individual to claim the protection of the laws whenever he receives an injury. One of the first duties of government is to afford that protection. . . .

The Government of the United States has been emphatically termed a government of laws, and not of men. It will certainly cease to deserve this high appellation if the laws furnish no remedy for the violation of a vested legal right. . . .

It behooves us, then, to inquire whether there be in its composition any ingredient which shall exempt from legal investigation or exclude the injured party from legal redress. In pursuing this inquiry, the first question which presents itself is whether this can be arranged with that class of cases which come under the description of *damnum absque injuria*— a loss without an injury.

This description of cases never has been considered, and, it is believed, never can be considered, as comprehending offices of trust, of honour or of profit. The office of justice of peace in the District of Columbia is such an office; it is therefore worthy of the attention and guardianship of the laws. . . . It is not then on account of the worthlessness of the thing pursued that the injured party can be alleged to be without remedy.

Is it in the nature of the transaction? Is the act of delivering or withholding a commission to be considered as a mere political act belonging to the Executive department alone, for the performance of which entire confidence is placed by our Constitution in the Supreme Executive, and for any misconduct respecting which the injured individual has no remedy?

That there may be such cases is not to be questioned. but that every act of duty to be performed in any of the great departments of government constitutes such a case is not to be admitted. . . .

It follows, then, that the question whether the legality of an act of the head of a department be examinable in a court of justice or not must always depend on the nature of that act. . . .

By the Constitution of the United States, the President is invested with certain important political powers, in the exercise of which he is to use his own discretion, and is accountable only to his country in his political character and to his own conscience. To aid him in the performance of these duties, he is authorized to appoint certain officers, who act by his authority and in conformity with his orders.

In such cases, their acts are his acts; and whatever opinion may be entertained of the manner in which executive discretion may be used, still there exists, and can exist, no power to control that discretion. The subjects are political. They respect the nation, not individual rights, and, being entrusted to the Executive, the decision of the Executive is conclusive. . . . The acts of such an officer, as an officer, can never be examinable by the Courts.

But when the Legislature proceeds to impose on that officer other duties; when he is directed peremptorily to perform certain acts; when the rights of individuals are dependent on the performance of those acts; he is so far the officer of the law, is amenable to the laws for his conduct, and cannot at his discretion, sport away the vested rights of others.

The conclusion from this reasoning is that, where the heads of departments are the political or confidential agents of the Executive, merely to execute the will of the President, or rather to act in cases in which the Executive possesses a constitutional or legal discretion, nothing can be more perfectly clear than that their acts are only politically examinable. But where a specific duty is assigned by law, and individual rights depend upon the performance of that duty, it seems equally clear that the individual who considers himself injured has a right to resort to the laws of his country for a remedy. . . .

It is then the opinion of the Court:

> 1. That, by signing the commission of Mr. Marbury, the President of the United States appointed him a justice of peace for the County of Washington in the District of Columbia, and that the seal of the United States, affixed thereto by the Secretary of State, is conclusive testimony of the verity of the signature, and of the completion of the appointment, and that the appointment conferred on him a legal right to the office for the space of five years.
> 2. That, having this legal title to the office, he has a consequent right to the commission, a refusal

to deliver which is a plain violation of that right, for which the laws of his country afford him a remedy.

It remains to be inquired whether,

3. He is entitled to the remedy for which he applies. This depends on:

> 1. The nature of the writ applied for, and
> 2. The power of this court. . . .

This . . . is a plain case of a mandamus, either to deliver the commission or a copy of it from the record, and it only remains to be inquired:

Whether it can issue from this Court.

The act to establish the judicial courts of the United States authorizes the Supreme Court "to issue writs of mandamus, in cases warranted by the principles and usages of law, to any courts appointed, or persons holding office, under the authority of the United States."

The Secretary of State, being a person, holding an office under the authority of the United States, is precisely within the letter of the description, and if this Court is not authorized to issue a writ of mandamus to such an officer, it must be because the law is unconstitutional, and therefore absolutely incapable of conferring the authority and assigning the duties which its words purport to confer and assign.

The Constitution vests the whole judicial power of the United States in one Supreme Court, and such inferior courts as Congress shall, from time to time, ordain and establish. This power is expressly extended to all cases arising under the laws of the United States; and consequently, in some form, may be exercised over the present case, because the right claimed is given by a law of the United States.

In the distribution of this power, it is declared that

"The Supreme Court shall have original jurisdiction in all cases affecting ambassadors, other public ministers and consuls, and those in which a state shall be a party. In all other cases, the Supreme Court shall have appellate jurisdiction." . . .

To enable this court then to issue a mandamus, it must be shown to be an exercise of appellate jurisdiction, or to be necessary to enable them to exercise appellate jurisdiction.

It has been stated at the bar that the appellate jurisdiction may be exercised in a variety of forms, and that, if it be the will of the Legislature that a mandamus should be used for that purpose, that will must be obeyed. This is true; yet the jurisdiction must be appellate, not original.

It is the essential criterion of appellate jurisdiction that it revises and corrects the proceedings in a cause already instituted, and does not create that case. Although, therefore, a mandamus may be directed to courts, yet to issue such a writ to an officer for the delivery of a paper is, in effect, the same as to sustain an original action for that paper, and therefore seems not to belong to appellate, but to original jurisdiction. Neither is it necessary in such a case as this to enable the Court to exercise its appellate jurisdiction.

The authority, therefore, given to the Supreme Court by the act establishing the judicial courts of the United States to issue writs of mandamus to public officers appears not to be warranted by the Constitution, and it becomes necessary to inquire whether a jurisdiction so conferred can be exercised.

The question whether an act repugnant to the Constitution can become the law of the land is a question deeply interesting to the United States, but, happily, not of an intricacy

proportioned to its interest. It seems only necessary to recog-
nise certain principles, supposed to have been long and well
established, to decide it.

That the people have an original right to establish for their
future government such principles as, in their opinion, shall
most conduce to their own happiness is the basis on which
the whole American fabric has been erected. The exercise of
this original right is a very great exertion; nor can it nor ought
it to be frequently repeated. The principles, therefore, so established are deemed fundamental. And as the authority
from which they proceed, is supreme, and can seldom act,
they are designed to be permanent.

This original and supreme will organizes the government
and assigns to different departments their respective powers.
It may either stop here or establish certain limits not to be
transcended by those departments.

The Government of the United States is of the latter
description. The powers of the Legislature are defined and
limited; and that those limits may not be mistaken or forgotten, the Constitution is written. To what purpose are powers
limited, and to what purpose is that limitation committed to
writing, if these limits may at any time be passed by those intended to be restrained? The distinction between a government with limited and unlimited powers is abolished if those
limits do not confine the persons on whom they are imposed,
and if acts prohibited and acts allowed are of equal obligation. It is a proposition too plain to be contested that the
Constitution controls any legislative act repugnant to it, or
that the Legislature may alter the Constitution by an ordinary act.

Between these alternatives there is no middle ground.
The Constitution is either a superior, paramount law, un-

changeable by ordinary means, or it is on a level with ordinary legislative acts, and, like other acts, is alterable when the legislature shall please to alter it.

If the former part . . . be true, then a legislative act contrary to the Constitution is not law; if the latter part be true, then written Constitutions are absurd attempts on the part of the people to limit a power in its own nature illimitable.

Certainly all those who have framed written Constitutions contemplate them as forming the fundamental and paramount law of the nation, and consequently the theory of every such government must be that an act of the Legislature repugnant to the Constitution is void.

This theory is essentially attached to a written Constitution, and is consequently to be considered by this Court as one of the fundamental principles of our society. It is not, therefore, to be lost sight of in the further consideration of this subject.

If an act of the Legislature repugnant to the Constitution is void, does it, notwithstanding its invalidity, bind the Courts and oblige them to give it effect? Or, in other words, though it be not law, does it constitute a rule as operative as if it was a law? This would be to overthrow in fact what was established in theory, and would seem, at first view, an absurdity too gross to be insisted on. It shall, however, receive a more attentive consideration.

It is emphatically the province and duty of the Judicial Department to say what the law is. Those who apply the rule to particular cases must, of necessity, expound and interpret that rule. If two laws conflict with each other, the Courts must decide on the operation of each.

So, if a law be in opposition to the Constitution, if both the law and the Constitution apply to a particular case, so that the Court must either decide that case conformably to the law, disregarding the Constitution, or conformably to the Constitution, disregarding the law, the Court must determine which of these conflicting rules governs the case. This is of the very essence of judicial duty.

If, then, the Courts are to regard the Constitution, and the Constitution is superior to any ordinary act of the Legislature, the Constitution, and not such ordinary act, must govern the case to which they both apply.

Those, then, who controvert the principle that the Constitution is to be considered in court as a paramount law are reduced to the necessity of maintaining that courts must close their eyes on the Constitution, and see only the law.

This doctrine would subvert the very foundation of all written Constitutions. It would declare that an act which, according to the principles and theory of our government, is entirely void, is yet, in practice, completely obligatory. It would declare that, if the Legislature shall do what is expressly forbidden, such act, notwithstanding the express prohibition, is in reality effectual. It would be giving to the Legislature a practical and real omnipotence with the same breath which professes to restrict their powers within narrow limits. It is prescribing limits, and declaring that those limits may be passed at pleasure.

That it thus reduces to nothing what we have deemed the greatest improvement on political institutions—a written Constitution, would of itself be sufficient, in America where written Constitutions have been viewed with so much reverence, for rejecting the construction. But the peculiar expressions of the Constitution of the United States furnish additional arguments in favour of its rejection. . . .

. . . [I]t is apparent that the framers of the Constitution

contemplated that instrument as a rule for the government of courts, as well as of the Legislature.

Why otherwise does it direct the judges to take an oath to support it? This oath certainly applies in an especial manner to their conduct in their official character. How immoral to impose it on them if they were to be used as the instruments, and the knowing instruments, for violating what they swear to support!

The oath of office, too, imposed by the Legislature, is completely demonstrative of the legislative opinion on this subject. It is in these words:

> "I do solemnly swear that I will administer justice without respect to persons, and do equal right to the poor and to the rich; and that I will faithfully and impartially discharge all the duties incumbent on me as according to the best of my abilities and understanding, agreeably to the Constitution and laws of the United States."

Why does a judge swear to discharge his duties agreeably to the Constitution of the United States if that Constitution forms no rule for his government? if it is closed upon him and cannot be inspected by him?

If such be the real state of things, this is worse than solemn mockery. To prescribe or to take this oath becomes equally a crime.

It is also not entirely unworthy of observation that, in declaring what shall be the supreme law of the land, the Constitution itself is first mentioned, and not the laws of the United States generally, but those only which shall be made in pursuance of the Constitution, have that rank.

Thus, the particular phraseology of the Constitution of the United States confirms and strengthens the principle, supposed to be essential to all written Constitutions, that a law repugnant to the Constitution is void, and that courts, as well as other departments, are bound by that instrument.

The rule must be discharged.

Part II

EQUAL PROTECTION

─────────── ☆ ───────────

This part of the volume demonstrates the role of the Supreme Court in enabling slavery and various forms of discrimination. In particular, it looks at now widely reviled cases such as *Dred Scott v. Sandford* and *Plessy v. Ferguson*. But it also details the Court's attempts to reverse its previous wrong decisions in these areas. Central to this part of the book is the meaning of equality under the Constitution. Pay particular attention to Justice Harlan's dissent in *Plessy*, as it foreshadows the Court's later course correction. Harlan's use of the term "color blindness" also sets the stage for the contemporary debate over whether affirmative action is consistent with the Constitution's requirement of "equal protection," highlighted in the excerpt from the Court's examination of the practice at the University of Michigan. While many of the Court's cases concerned the issue of discrimination against Black Americans, this part also highlights discrimination based on undocumented status (*Plyler v. Doe*) and discrimination against Asian Americans (*Yick Wo v. Hopkins*, *Chae Chan Ping v. United States*, and *Korematsu v. United States*). As you will see, the Court's record has been mixed when it comes to such discrimination.

Dred Scott v. Sandford
(1857)

> *In this case, the Supreme Court ruled that Black people,
> enslaved or free, were not citizens under the Constitu-
> tion. In doing so, the Court argued that the liberties con-
> tained in the Constitution did not extend to Black
> people.*

Mr. Chief Justice TANEY delivered the opinion of the
court. . . .

There are two leading questions presented by the record:

> 1. Had the Circuit Court of the United States
> jurisdiction to hear and determine the case be-
> tween these parties? And
> 2. If it had jurisdiction, is the judgment it has
> given erroneous or not?

The plaintiff in error, who was also the plaintiff in the
court below, was, with his wife and children, held as slaves
by the defendant in the State of Missouri, and he brought this
action in the Circuit Court of the United States for that district to assert the title of himself and his family to freedom.

The declaration is in the form usually adopted in that State to try questions of this description, and contains the averment necessary to give the court jurisdiction; that he and the defendant are citizens of different States; that is, that he is a citizen of Missouri, and the defendant a citizen of New York.

The defendant pleaded in abatement to the jurisdiction of the court, that the plaintiff was not a citizen of the State of Missouri, as alleged in his declaration, being a negro of African descent, whose ancestors were of pure African blood and who were brought into this country and sold as slaves. . . .

. . . [I]t becomes, therefore, our duty to decide whether the facts stated in the plea are or are not sufficient to show that the plaintiff is not entitled to sue as a citizen in a court of the United States.

This is certainly a very serious question, and one that now for the first time has been brought for decision before this court. But it is brought here by those who have a right to bring it, and it is our duty to meet it and decide it.

The question is simply this: can a negro whose ancestors were imported into this country and sold as slaves become a member of the political community formed and brought into existence by the Constitution of the United States, and as such become entitled to all the rights, and privileges, and immunities, guarantied by that instrument to the citizen, one of which rights is the privilege of suing in a court of the United States in the cases specified in the Constitution?

It will be observed that the plea applies to that class of persons only whose ancestors were negroes of the African race, and imported into this country and sold and held as slaves. The only matter in issue before the court, therefore, is, whether the descendants of such slaves, when they shall be emancipated, or who are born of parents who had become free before their birth, are citizens of a State in the sense in which the word "citizen" is used in the Constitution of the United States. . . .

. . . We think they are not, and that they are not included, and were not intended to be included, under the word "citizens" in the Constitution, and can therefore claim none of the rights and privileges which that instrument provides for and secures to citizens of the United States. . . .

In the opinion of the court, the legislation and histories of the times, and the language used in the Declaration of Independence, show that neither the class of persons who had been imported as slaves nor their descendants, whether they had become free or not, were then acknowledged as a part of the people, nor intended to be included in the general words used in that memorable instrument. . . .

They had for more than a century before been regarded as beings of an inferior order, and altogether unfit to associate with the white race either in social or political relations, and so far inferior that they had no rights which the white man was bound to respect, and that the negro might justly and lawfully be reduced to slavery for his benefit. . . .

The legislation of the different colonies furnishes positive and indisputable proof of this fact. . . .

. . . They show that a perpetual and impassable barrier was intended to be erected between the white race and the one which they had reduced to slavery, and governed as subjects with absolute and despotic power, and which they then looked upon as so far below them in the scale of created beings, that intermarriages between white persons and negroes or mulattoes were regarded as unnatural and immoral, and punished as crimes, not only in the parties, but in the person who joined them in marriage. And no distinction in this respect was made between the free negro or mulatto and the slave, but this stigma of the deepest degradation was fixed upon the whole race. . . .

The language of the Declaration of Independence is equally conclusive: . . .

> "We hold these truths to be self-evident: that all men are created equal; that they are endowed by their Creator with certain unalienable rights; that among them is life, liberty, and the pursuit of happiness; that to secure these rights, Governments are instituted, deriving their just powers from the consent of the governed."

The general words above quoted would seem to embrace the whole human family, and if they were used in a similar instrument at this day would be so understood. But it is too clear for dispute that the enslaved African race were not intended to be included, and formed no part of the people who framed and adopted this declaration, for if the language, as understood in that day, would embrace them, the conduct of the distinguished men who framed the Declaration of Independence would have been utterly and flagrantly inconsistent with the principles they asserted, and instead of the sympathy of mankind to which they so confidently appealed, they would have deserved and received universal rebuke and reprobation.

Yet the men who framed this declaration were great men—high in literary acquirements, high in their sense of honor, and incapable of asserting principles inconsistent with those on which they were acting. . . . The unhappy black race were separated from the white by indelible marks, and laws long before established, and were never thought of or spoken of except as property, and when the claims of the owner or the profit of the trader were supposed to need protection.

This state of public opinion had undergone no change when the Constitution was adopted, as is equally evident from its provisions and language. . . .

. . . More especially, it cannot be believed that the large slaveholding States regarded them as included in the word citizens, or would have consented to a Constitution which might compel them to receive them in that character from another State. For if they were so received, and entitled to the privileges and immunities of citizens, it would exempt them from the operation of the special laws and from the police regulations which they considered to be necessary for their own safety. . . .

No one, we presume, supposes that any change in public opinion or feeling, in relation to this unfortunate race, in the civilized nations of Europe or in this country, should induce the court to give to the words of the Constitution a more liberal construction in their favor than they were intended to bear when the instrument was framed and adopted. Such an argument would be altogether inadmissible in any tribunal called on to interpret it. If any of its provisions are deemed unjust, there is a mode prescribed in the instrument itself by which it may be amended; but while it remains unaltered, it must be construed now as it was understood at the time of its adoption. . . .

And, upon a full and careful consideration of the subject, the court is of opinion, that, upon the facts stated in the plea in abatement, Dred Scott was not a citizen of Missouri within the meaning of the Constitution of the United States, and not entitled as such to sue in its courts, and consequently that the Circuit Court had no jurisdiction of the case, and that the judgment on the plea in abatement is erroneous. . . .

Yick Wo v. Hopkins
(1886)

In this case, the Supreme Court ruled that a law that did not explicitly discriminate on the basis of national origin still violated the Equal Protection Clause of the Fourteenth Amendment because it was discriminatorily applied.

. . . These two cases were argued as one, and depended upon precisely the same state of facts; the first coming here upon a writ of error to the Supreme Court of the State of California, the second on appeal from the Circuit Court of the United States for that district. The plaintiff in error, Yick Wo, on August 4, 1885, petitioned the Supreme Court of California for a writ of habeas corpus, alleging that he was illegally deprived of his personal liberty by the defendant as sheriff of the city and county of San Francisco.

The sheriff made return to the writ that he held the petitioner in custody by virtue of a sentence of the Police Judges Court, No. 2, of the city and county of San Francisco, whereby he was found guilty of a violation of certain ordinances. . . .

The ordinances for the violation of which he had been found guilty were set out as follows:

Order No. 156, passed May 26, 1880, prescribing the kind of buildings in which laundries may be located. . . .

Order No. 1587, passed July 28, 1880, the following section:

> "SEC. 68. It shall be unlawful, from and after the passage of this order, for any person or persons to establish, maintain, or carry on a laundry within the corporate limits of the city and county of San Francisco without having first obtained the consent of the board of supervisors, except the same be located in a building constructed either of brick or stone."

The following facts were also admitted on the record: that petitioner is a native of China and came to California in 1861, and is still a subject of the Emperor of China; that he has been engaged in the laundry business in the same premises and building for twenty-two years last past; that he had a license from the board of fire wardens, dated March 3, 1884, from which it appeared

> "that the above described premises have been inspected by the board of fire wardens, and upon such inspection said board found all proper arrangements for carrying on the business; . . . that he had a certificate from the health officer that the same premises had been inspected by him, and that he found that they were properly and sufficiently drained, and that all proper arrangements for carrying on the business of a laundry . . . had been complied with; that the city license of the petitioner was in

force and expired October 1st, 1885, and that the petitioner applied to the board of supervisors, June 1st, 1885,
for consent of said board to maintain and carry on his
laundry, but that said board, on July 1st, 1885, refused
said consent." . . .

It was alleged in the petition, that

"Your petitioner and more than one hundred and fifty
of his countrymen have been arrested upon the charge
of carrying on business without having such special
consent, while those who are not subjects of China,
and who are conducting eighty odd laundries under
similar conditions, are left unmolested and free to
enjoy the enhanced trade and profits arising from this
hurtful and unfair discrimination. The business of
your petitioner, and of those of his countrymen similarly situated, is greatly impaired, and in many cases
practically ruined, by this system of oppression to one
kind of men and favoritism to all others." . . .

Mr. JUSTICE MATTHEWS delivered the opinion of the
court.

In the case of the petitioner, brought here by writ of error
to the Supreme Court of California, our jurisdiction is limited to the question whether the plaintiff in error has been
denied a right in violation of the Constitution, laws, or treaties of the United States. . . .

We are consequently constrained, at the outset, to differ
from the Supreme Court of California upon the real meaning of the ordinances in question. That court considered these
ordinances as vesting in the board of supervisors a not unusual

discretion in granting or withholding their assent to the use of wooden buildings as laundries, to be exercised in reference to the circumstances of each case with a view to the protection of the public against the dangers of fire. We are not able to concur in that interpretation of the power conferred upon the supervisors. There is nothing in the ordinances which points to such a regulation of the business of keeping and conducting laundries. They seem intended to confer, and actually do confer, not a discretion to be exercised upon a consideration of the circumstances of each case, but a naked and arbitrary power to give or withhold consent not only as to places, but as to persons. . . .

The rights of the petitioners, as affected by the proceedings of which they complain, are not less because they are aliens and subjects of the Emperor of China. . . .

The Fourteenth Amendment to the Constitution is not confined to the protection of citizens. It says:

> "Nor shall any State deprive any person of life, liberty, or property without due process of law; nor deny to any person within its jurisdiction the equal protection of the laws."

These provisions are universal in their application to all persons within the territorial jurisdiction, without regard to any differences of race, of color, or of nationality, and the equal protection of the laws is a pledge of the protection of equal laws. . . .

The questions we have to consider and decide in these cases, therefore, are to be treated as invoking the rights of every citizen of the United States equally with those of the strangers and aliens who now invoke the jurisdiction of the court. . . .

When we consider the nature and the theory of our institutions of government, the principles upon which they are supposed to rest, and review the history of their development, we are constrained to conclude that they do not mean to leave room for the play and action of purely personal and arbitrary power. Sovereignty itself is, of course, not subject to law, for it is the author and source of law; but, in our system, while sovereign powers are delegated to the agencies of government, sovereignty itself remains with the people, by whom and for whom all government exists and acts. And the law is the definition and limitation of power. It is, indeed, quite true that there must always be lodged somewhere, and in some person or body, the authority of final decision, and in many cases of mere administration, the responsibility is purely political, no appeal lying except to the ultimate tribunal of the public judgment, exercised either in the pressure of opinion or by means of the suffrage. But the fundamental rights to life, liberty, and the pursuit of happiness, considered as individual possessions, are secured by those maxims of constitutional law which are the monuments showing the victorious progress of the race in securing to men the blessings of civilization under the reign of just and equal laws, so that, in the famous language of the Massachusetts Bill of Rights, the government of the commonwealth "may be a government of laws, and not of men." For the very idea that one man may be compelled to hold his life, or the means of living, or any material right essential to the enjoyment of life at the mere will of another seems to be intolerable in any country where freedom prevails, as being the essence of slavery itself. . . .

. . . Though the law itself be fair on its face and impartial in appearance, yet, if it is applied and administered by public authority with an evil eye and an unequal hand, so as practically to make unjust and illegal discriminations between persons in similar circumstances, material to their rights, the denial of equal justice is still within the prohibition of the Constitution. . . .

The present cases, as shown by the facts disclosed in the record, are within this class. It appears that both petitioners have complied with every requisite deemed by the law or by the public officers charged with its administration necessary for the protection of neighboring property from fire or as a precaution against injury to the public health. No reason whatever, except the will of the supervisors, is assigned why they should not be permitted to carry on, in the accustomed manner, their harmless and useful occupation, on which they depend for a livelihood. And while this consent of the supervisors is withheld from them and from two hundred others who have also petitioned, all of whom happen to be Chinese subjects, eighty others, not Chinese subjects, are permitted to carry on the same business under similar conditions. The fact of this discrimination is admitted. No reason for it is shown, and the conclusion cannot be resisted that no reason for it exists except hostility to the race and nationality to which the petitioners belong, and which, in the eye of the law, is not justified. The discrimination is, therefore, illegal, and the public administration which enforces it is a denial of the equal protection of the laws and a violation of the Fourteenth Amendment of the Constitution. The imprisonment of the petitioners is, therefore, illegal, and they must be discharged. . . .

Chae Chan Ping v. United States
(1889)

This landmark immigration case upheld the constitutionality of part of the Chinese Exclusion Act. The case established a key tenet of the plenary power doctrine, which gives the two political branches of government wide latitude in creating immigration and national security policies. At the same time, it vastly limited the rights of noncitizen residents once they left the country.

MR. JUSTICE FIELD delivered the opinion of the Court.

The appeal involves a consideration of the validity of the Act of Congress of October 1, 1888, prohibiting Chinese laborers from entering the United States who had departed before its passage, having a certificate issued . . . granting them permission to return. The validity of the act is assailed as being in effect an expulsion from the country of Chinese laborers, in violation of existing treaties between the United States and the government of China, and of rights vested in them under the laws of Congress. . . .

Neither the treaty of 1844 nor that of 1858 touched upon the migration and emigration of the citizens and subjects of the two nations, respectively, from one country to the other.

But in 1868 a great change in the relations of the two nations was made in that respect. In that year a mission from China, composed of distinguished functionaries of that empire, came to the United States with the professed object of establishing closer relations between the two countries and their peoples. . . . On its arrival in Washington, additional articles to the treaty of 1858 were agreed upon, which gave expression to the general desire that the two nations and their peoples should be drawn closer together. The new articles, eight in number, were agreed to on the 28th of July, 1868, and ratifications of them were exchanged at Pekin in November of the following year. Of these articles, the fifth, sixth, and seventh are as follows:

> "ARTICLE V. The United States of America and the emperor of China cordially recognize the inherent and inalienable right of man to change his home and allegiance, and also the mutual advantage of the free migration and emigration of their citizens and subjects respectively from the one country to the other for purposes of curiosity, of trade, or as permanent residents. . . .
>
> ARTICLE VI. Citizens of the United States visiting or residing in China shall enjoy the same privileges, immunities, or exemptions in respect to travel or residence as may there be enjoyed by the citizens or subjects of the most favored nation; and, reciprocally, Chinese subjects visiting or residing in the United shall enjoy the same privileges, immunities, and exemptions. . . .
>
> ARTICLE VII. Citizens of the United States shall enjoy all the privileges of the public educational institutions under the control of the government of China,

> and, reciprocally, Chinese subjects shall enjoy all the privileges of the public educational institutions under the control of the government of the United States, which are enjoyed in the respective countries by the citizens or subjects of the most favored nation. . . ."

But notwithstanding these strong expressions of friendship and goodwill, and the desire they evince for free intercourse, events were transpiring on the Pacific coast which soon dissipated the anticipations indulged as to the benefits to follow the immigration of Chinese to this country. . . . Whatever modifications have since been made to these general provisions have been caused by a well-founded apprehension—from the experience of years—that a limitation to the immigration of certain classes from China was essential to the peace of the community on the Pacific coast, and possibly to the preservation of our civilization there. . . .

The discovery of gold in California in 1848, as is well known, was followed by a large immigration thither from all parts of the world, attracted not only by the hope of gain from the mines, but from the great prices paid for all kinds of labor. The news of the discovery penetrated China, and laborers came from there in great numbers, a few with their own means, but by far the greater number under contract with employers, for whose benefit they worked. These laborers readily secured employment, and, as domestic servants, and in various kinds of outdoor work, proved to be exceedingly useful. For some years little opposition was made to them, except when they sought to work in the mines, but, as their numbers increased, they began to engage in various mechanical pursuits and trades, and thus came in competition with our artisans and mechanics, as well as our laborers in the field. . . . The competition between them and our people was for this reason altogether in their favor, and the consequent irritation, proportionately deep and bitter, was followed, in many cases, by open conflicts, to the great disturbance of the public peace.

The differences of race added greatly to the difficulties of the situation. Notwithstanding the favorable provisions of the new articles of the treaty of 1868, by which all the privileges, immunities, and exemptions were extended to subjects of China in the United States which were accorded to citizens or subjects of the most favored nation, they remained strangers in the land, residing apart by themselves, and adhering to the customs and usages of their own country. It seemed impossible for them to assimilate with our people, or to make any change in their habits or modes of living. As they grew in numbers each year the people of the coast saw, or believed they saw, in the facility of immigration, and in the crowded millions of China, where population presses upon the means of subsistence, great danger that at no distant day that portion of our country would be overrun by them, unless prompt action was taken to restrict their immigration. The people there accordingly petitioned earnestly for protective legislation. . . .

. . . A statute was accordingly passed appropriating money to send commissioners to China to act with our minister there in negotiating and concluding by treaty a settlement of such matters of interest between the two governments as might be confided to them. Such commissioners were appointed, and as the result of their negotiations the supplementary treaty of November 17, 1880, was concluded and ratified in May of the following year. . . .

The government of China thus agreed that, notwithstanding the stipulations of former treaties, the United States might regulate, limit, or suspend the coming of Chinese laborers, or their residence therein, without absolutely forbidding it, whenever in their opinion the interests of the country, or of any part of it, might require such action. Legislation for such regulation, limitation, or suspension was entrusted to the discretion of our government, with the condition that it should only be such as might be necessary for that purpose, and that the immigrants should not be maltreated or abused. On the 6th of May, 1882, an act of Congress was approved, to carry this supplementary treaty into effect. It is entitled "An act to execute certain treaty stipulations relating to Chinese." Its first section declares that after 90 days from the passage of the act, and for the period of 10 years from its date, the coming of Chinese laborers to the United States is suspended, and that it shall be unlawful for any such laborer to come, or, having come, to remain within the United States. . . . The fourth declares that, for the purpose of identifying the laborers . . . to furnish them with "the proper evidence" of their right to go from and come to the United States, . . . and each laborer thus departing shall be entitled to receive, from the collector or his deputy, a certificate containing such particulars, corresponding with the registry, as may serve to identify him. "The certificate herein provided for," says the section, "shall entitle the Chinese laborer to whom the same is issued to return to and reenter the United States upon producing and delivering the same to the collector of customs of the district at which such Chinese laborer shall seek to re-enter."

The enforcement of this act with respect to laborers who were in the United States on November 17, 1880, was attended with great embarrassment, from the suspicious nature, in many instances, of the testimony offered to establish the residence of the parties, arising from the loose notions entertained by the witnesses of the obligation of an oath. . . .

. . . To prevent the possibility of the policy of excluding Chinese laborers being evaded, the act of October 1, 1888, the validity of which is the subject of consideration in this case, was passed. . . . It is as follows:

> *"Be it enacted by the Senate and House of Representatives of the United States of America, in Congress assembled*, that from and after the passage of this act it shall be unlawful for any Chinese laborer who shall at any time heretofore have been, or who may now or hereafter be, a resident within the United States, and who shall have departed, or shall depart, therefrom, and shall not have returned before the passage of this act, to return to or remain the United States."
>
> "SEC. 2. That no certificates of identity provided for in the fourth and fifth sections of the act to which this is a supplement shall hereafter be issued; and every certificate heretofore issued in pursuance thereof is hereby declared void and of no effect. . . ."

The validity of this act, as already mentioned, is assailed, as being in effect an expulsion from the country of Chinese laborers, in violation of existing treaties between the United States and the government of China, and of rights vested in them under the laws of Congress. . . .

. . . That the government of the United States, through the action of the legislative department, can exclude aliens from its territory is a proposition which we do not think open to controversy. Jurisdiction over its own territory to that extent is an incident of every independent nation. It is a part of its independence. If it could not exclude aliens it would be to that extent subject to the control of another power. . . .

While under our Constitution and form of government the great mass of local matters is controlled by local authorities, the United States, in their relation to foreign countries and their subjects or citizens, are one nation, invested with powers which belong to independent nations, the exercise of which can be invoked for the maintenance of its absolute independence and security throughout its entire territory. The powers to declare war, make treaties, suppress insurrection, repel invasion, regulate foreign commerce, secure republican governments to the states, and admit subjects of other nations to citizenship, are all sovereign powers, restricted in their exercise only by the Constitution itself and considerations of public policy and justice which control, more or less, the conduct of all civilized nations. . . .

To preserve its independence, and give security against foreign aggression and encroachment, is the highest duty of every nation, and to attain these ends nearly all other considerations are to be subordinated. It matters not in what form such aggression and encroachment come, whether from the foreign nation acting in its national character, or from vast hordes of its people crowding in upon us. . . . If, therefore, the government of the United States, through its legislative department, considers the presence of foreigners of a different race in this country, who will not assimilate with us, to be dangerous to its peace and security, their exclusion is not to be stayed because at the time there are no actual hostilities with the nation of which the foreigners are subjects. . . .

The power of exclusion of foreigners being an incident of sovereignty belonging to the government of the United States as a part of those sovereign powers delegated by the Constitution, the right to its exercise at any time when, in the judgment of the government, the interests of the country require it, cannot be granted away or restrained on behalf of anyone.

. . . Whether a proper consideration by our government of its previous laws, or a proper respect for the nation whose subjects are affected by its action, ought to have qualified its inhibition, and made it applicable only to persons departing from the country after the passage of the act, are not questions for judicial determination. . . .

Order affirmed.

Plessy v. Ferguson
(1896)

> *In one of its most misguided decisions, the Supreme Court upheld the constitutionality of racial segregation and established the "separate but equal" doctrine. It ruled that public facilities could be segregated on the basis of race provided that the facilities were equal in quality.*

MR. JUSTICE BROWN, after stating the case, delivered the opinion of the court.

This case turns upon the constitutionality of an act of the General Assembly of the State of Louisiana, passed in 1890, providing for separate railway carriages for the white and colored races. . . .

The information filed in the criminal District Court charged in substance that Plessy, being a passenger between two stations within the State of Louisiana, was assigned by officers of the company to the coach used for the race to which he belonged, but he insisted upon going into a coach used by the race to which he did not belong. . . . The petition for the writ of prohibition averred that petitioner was seven-eighths Caucasian and one eighth African blood; that the mixture of colored blood was not discernible in him, and that he was entitled to every right, privilege and immunity secured to citizens of the United States of the white race; and that, upon such theory, he took possession of a vacant seat in a coach where passengers of the white race were accommodated, and was ordered by the conductor to vacate said coach and take a seat in another assigned to persons of the colored race, and, having refused to comply with such demand, he was forcibly ejected with the aid of a police officer, and imprisoned in the parish jail to answer a charge of having violated the above act.

The constitutionality of this act is attacked upon the ground that it conflicts both with the Thirteenth Amendment of the Constitution, abolishing slavery, and the Fourteenth Amendment, which prohibits certain restrictive legislation on the part of the States.

1. That it does not conflict with the Thirteenth Amendment, which abolished slavery and involuntary servitude, except as a punishment for crime, is too clear for argument. Slavery implies involuntary servitude—a state of bondage; the ownership of mankind as a chattel, or at least the control of the labor and services of one man for the benefit of another, and the absence of a legal right to the disposal of his own person, property and services. . . .

A statute which implies merely a legal distinction between the white and colored races—a distinction which is founded in the color of the two races and which must always exist so long as white men are distinguished from the other race by color—has no tendency to destroy the legal equality of the two races, or reestablish a state of involuntary servitude. Indeed, we do not understand that the Thirteenth Amendment is strenuously relied upon by the plaintiff in error in this connection.

2. By the Fourteenth Amendment, all persons born or

naturalized in the United States and subject to the jurisdiction thereof are made citizens of the United States and of the State wherein they reside, and the States are forbidden from making or enforcing any law which shall abridge the privileges or immunities of citizens of the United States, or shall deprive any person of life, liberty, or property without due process of law, or deny to any person within their jurisdiction the equal protection of the laws. . . .

The object of the amendment was undoubtedly to enforce the absolute equality of the two races before the law, but, in the nature of things, it could not have been intended to abolish distinctions based upon color, or to enforce social, as distinguished from political, equality, or a commingling of the two races upon terms unsatisfactory to either. Laws permitting, and even requiring, their separation in places where they are liable to be brought into contact do not necessarily imply the inferiority of either race to the other, and have been generally, if not universally, recognized as within the competency of the state legislatures in the exercise of their police power. The most common instance of this is connected with the establishment of separate schools for white and colored children, which has been held to be a valid exercise of the legislative power even by courts of States where the political rights of the colored race have been longest and most earnestly enforced. . . .

It is claimed by the plaintiff in error that, in any mixed community, the reputation of belonging to the dominant race, in this instance the white race, is property in the same sense that a right of action or of inheritance is property. Conceding this to be so for the purposes of this case, we are unable to see how this statute deprives him of, or in any way affects his right to, such property. If he be a white man and assigned to a colored coach, he may have his action for damages against the company for being deprived of his so-called property. Upon the other hand, if he be a colored man and be so assigned, he has been deprived of no property, since he is not lawfully entitled to the reputation of being a white man.

In this connection, it is also suggested by the learned counsel for the plaintiff in error that the same argument that will justify the state legislature in requiring railways to provide separate accommodations for the two races will also authorize them to require separate cars to be provided for people whose hair is of a certain color, or who are aliens, or who belong to certain nationalities, or to enact laws requiring colored people to walk upon one side of the street and white people upon the other, or requiring white men's houses to be painted white and colored men's black, or their vehicles or business signs to be of different colors, upon the theory that one side of the street is as good as the other, or that a house or vehicle of one color is as good as one of another color. The reply to all this is that every exercise of the police power must be reasonable, and extend only to such laws as are enacted in good faith for the promotion for the public good, and not for the annoyance or oppression of a particular class. . . .

So far, then, as a conflict with the Fourteenth Amendment is concerned, the case reduces itself to the question whether the statute of Louisiana is a reasonable regulation, and, with respect to this, there must necessarily be a large discretion on the part of the legislature. In determining the question of reasonableness, it is at liberty to act with reference to the established usages, customs, and traditions of the people, and with a view to the promotion of their comfort and the preservation of the public peace and good order. Gauged by this standard, we cannot say that a law which authorizes or even requires the separation of the two races in public conveyances is unreasonable, or more obnoxious to the Fourteenth Amendment than the acts of Congress requiring separate schools for colored children in the District of Columbia, the constitutionality of which does not seem to have been questioned, or the corresponding acts of state legislatures.

We consider the underlying fallacy of the plaintiff's argument to consist in the assumption that the enforced separation of the two races stamps the colored race with a badge of inferiority. If this be so, it is not by reason of anything found in the act, but solely because the colored race chooses to put that construction upon it. The argument necessarily assumes that if, as has been more than once the case and is not unlikely to be so again, the colored race should become the dominant power in the state legislature, and should enact a law in precisely similar terms, it would thereby relegate the white race to an inferior position. We imagine that the white race, at least, would not acquiesce in this assumption. The argument also assumes that social prejudices may be overcome by legislation, and that equal rights cannot be secured to the negro except by an enforced commingling of the two races. We cannot accept this proposition. If the two races are to meet upon terms of social equality, it must be the result of natural affinities, a mutual appreciation of each other's merits, and a voluntary consent of individuals. . . .

Legislation is powerless to eradicate racial instincts or to abolish distinctions based upon physical differences, and the attempt to do so can only result in accentuating the difficulties of the present situation. If the civil and political rights of both races be equal, one cannot be inferior to the other civilly or politically. If one race be inferior to the other socially, the Constitution of the United States cannot put them upon the same plane.

It is true that the question of the proportion of colored

blood necessary to constitute a colored person, as distinguished from a white person, is one upon which there is a difference of opinion in the different States, some holding that any visible admixture of black blood stamps the person as belonging to the colored race; others that it depends upon the preponderance of blood; and still others that the predominance of white blood must only be in the proportion of three-fourths. But these are questions to be determined under the laws of each State, and are not properly put in issue in this case. Under the allegations of his petition, it may undoubtedly become a question of importance whether, under the laws of Louisiana, the petitioner belongs to the white or colored race.

The judgment of the court below is, therefore,

Affirmed.

United States v. Wong Kim Ark
(1898)

> *This case clarified the concept of birthright citizenship,*
> *guaranteed by the Fourteenth Amendment. The Court ruled*
> *that children born on American soil are automatically*
> *citizens of the United States, even if their parents are not.*

MR. JUSTICE GRAY, after stating the case, delivered the opinion of the court.

The facts of this case, as agreed by the parties, are as follows: Wong Kim Ark was born in 1873 in the city of San Francisco, in the State of California and United States of America, and was and is a laborer. His father and mother were persons of Chinese descent, and subjects of the Emperor of China. . . . Wong Kim Ark, ever since his birth, has had but one residence, in California, within the United States, and has there resided, claiming to be a citizen of the United States, and has never lost or changed that residence, or gained or acquired another residence, and neither he nor his parents acting for him ever renounced his allegiance to the United States, or did or committed any act or thing to exclude him therefrom. . . . [H]e remained in the United States, claiming to be a citizen thereof, until 1894, when he . . . again departed for China on a temporary visit and with the intention of returning to the United States, and he did return thereto by sea in August, 1895, and applied to the collector of customs for permission to land, and was denied such permission upon the sole ground that he was not a citizen of the United States.

It is conceded that, if he is a citizen of the United States, the acts of Congress, known as the Chinese Exclusion Acts, prohibiting persons of the Chinese race, and especially Chinese laborers, from coming into the United States, do not and cannot apply to him.

The question presented by the record is whether a child born in the United States, of parents of Chinese descent, who, at the time of his birth, are subjects of the Emperor of China, but have a permanent domicil and residence in the United States, and are there carrying on business, and are not employed in any diplomatic or official capacity under the Emperor of China, becomes at the time of his birth a citizen of the United States by virtue of the first clause of the Fourteenth Amendment of the Constitution,

> "All persons born or naturalized in the United States, and subject to the jurisdiction thereof, are citizens of the United States and of the State wherein they reside."

As appears upon the face of the amendment, as well as from the history of the times, this was not intended to impose any new restrictions upon citizenship, or to prevent any persons from becoming citizens by the fact of birth within the United States who would thereby have become citizens according to the law existing before its adoption. It is declaratory in form, and enabling and extending in effect. Its main purpose doubtless was, as has been often recognized by this court, to establish the citizenship of free negroes, which had been denied in the opinion delivered by Chief Justice Taney in *Dred Scott v. Sandford*, (1857), and to put it beyond doubt that all blacks, as well as whites, born or naturalized within the jurisdiction of the United States are citizens of the United States. But the opening words, "All persons born," are general, not to say universal, restricted only by place and jurisdiction, and not by color or race—as was clearly recognized in all the opinions delivered in *The Slaughterhouse Cases*. . . .

The real object of the Fourteenth Amendment of the Constitution, in qualifying the words, "All persons born in the United States" by the addition "and subject to the jurisdiction thereof," would appear to have been to exclude, by the fewest and fittest words (besides children of members of the Indian tribes, standing in a peculiar relation to the National Government, unknown to the common law), the two classes of cases—children born of alien enemies in hostile occupation and children of diplomatic representatives of a foreign State—both of which, as has already been shown, by the law of England and by our own law from the time of the first settlement of the English colonies in America, had been recognized exceptions to the fundamental rule of citizenship by birth within the country. . . .

These considerations confirm the view, already expressed in this opinion, that the opening sentence of the Fourteenth Amendment is throughout affirmative and declaratory, intended to allay doubts and to settle controversies which had arisen, and not to impose any new restrictions upon citizenship. . . .

The foregoing considerations and authorities irresistibly lead us to these conclusions: the Fourteenth Amendment affirms the ancient and fundamental rule of citizenship by birth within the territory, in the allegiance and under the protection of the country, including all children here born of resident aliens, with the exceptions or qualifications (as old as the rule itself) of children of foreign sovereigns or their ministers, or born on foreign public ships, or of enemies within and during a hostile occupation of part of our territory, and with the single additional exception of children of members of the Indian tribes owing direct allegiance to their several tribes. The Amendment, in clear words and in manifest intent, includes the children born, within the territory of the United States, of all other persons, of whatever race or color, domiciled within the United States. Every citizen or subject of another country, while domiciled here, is within the allegiance and the protection, and consequently subject to the jurisdiction, of the United States. His allegiance to the United States is direct and immediate. . . .

To hold that the Fourteenth Amendment of the Constitution excludes from citizenship the children, born in the United States, of citizens or subjects of other countries would be to deny citizenship to thousands of persons of English, Scotch, Irish, German, or other European parentage who have always been considered and treated as citizens of the United States.

VI. Whatever considerations, in the absence of a controlling provision of the Constitution, might influence the legislative or the executive branch of the Government to decline to admit persons of the Chinese race to the status of citizens of the United States, there are none that can constrain or permit the judiciary to refuse to give full effect to the peremptory and explicit language of the Fourteenth Amendment, which declares and ordains that "All persons born or naturalized in the United States, and subject to the jurisdiction thereof, are citizens of the United States."

Chinese persons, born out of the United States, remaining

subjects of the Emperor of China, and not having become citizens of the United States, are entitled to the protection of, and owe allegiance to, the United States so long as they are permitted by the United States to reside here, and are "subject to the jurisdiction thereof" in the same sense as all other aliens residing in the United States. . . .

The fact, therefore, that acts of Congress or treaties have not permitted Chinese persons born out of this country to become citizens by naturalization, cannot exclude Chinese persons born in this country from the operation of the broad and clear words of the Constitution, "All persons born in the United States, and subject to the jurisdiction thereof, are citizens of the United States."

VII. Upon the facts agreed in this case, the American citizenship which Wong Kim Ark acquired by birth within the United States has not been lost or taken away by anything happening since his birth. No doubt he might himself, after coming of age, renounce this citizenship and become a citizen of the country of his parents, or of any other country; for, by our law, as solemnly declared by Congress, "the right of expatriation is a natural and inherent right of all people," and

"any declaration, instruction, opinion, order or direction of any officer of the United States which denies, restricts, impairs or questions the right of expatriation, is declared inconsistent with the fundamental principles of the Republic." . . .

Order affirmed.

Korematsu v. United States
(1944)

One of the most infamous Supreme Court decisions, Korematsu upheld the constitutionality of Japanese internment camps during World War II.

MR. JUSTICE BLACK delivered the opinion of the Court.

The petitioner, an American citizen of Japanese descent, was convicted in a federal district court for remaining in San Leandro, California, a "Military Area," contrary to Civilian Exclusion Order No. 34 of the Commanding General of the Western Command, U.S. Army, which directed that, after May 9, 1942, all persons of Japanese ancestry should be excluded from that area. No question was raised as to petitioner's loyalty to the United States. . . .

It should be noted, to begin with, that all legal restrictions which curtail the civil rights of a single racial group are immediately suspect. That is not to say that all such restrictions are unconstitutional. It is to say that courts must subject them to the most rigid scrutiny. Pressing public necessity may sometimes justify the existence of such restrictions; racial antagonism never can. . . .

Exclusion Order No. 34, which the petitioner knowingly

and admittedly violated, was one of a number of military orders and proclamations, all of which were substantially based upon Executive Order No. 9066. That order, issued after we were at war with Japan, declared that

> "the successful prosecution of the war requires every possible protection against espionage and against sabotage to national defense material, national defense premises, and national defense utilities. . . ."

One of the series of orders and proclamations, a curfew order, which, like the exclusion order here, was promulgated pursuant to Executive Order 9066, subjected all persons of Japanese ancestry in prescribed West Coast military areas to remain in their residences from 8 p.m. to 6 a.m. As is the case with the exclusion order here, that prior curfew order was designed as a "protection against espionage and against sabotage." In *Hirabayashi v. United States*, we sustained a conviction obtained for violation of the curfew order. The Hirabayashi conviction and this one thus rest on the same 1942 Congressional Act and the same basic executive and military orders, all of which orders were aimed at the twin dangers of espionage and sabotage.

The 1942 Act was attacked in the *Hirabayashi* case as an unconstitutional delegation of power; it was contended that the curfew order and other orders on which it rested were beyond the war powers of the Congress, the military authorities, and of the President, as Commander in Chief of the Army, and, finally, that to apply the curfew order against none but citizens of Japanese ancestry amounted to a constitutionally prohibited discrimination solely on account of race. To these questions, we gave the serious consideration which their importance justified. We upheld the curfew order as an exercise of the power of the government to take steps necessary to prevent espionage and sabotage in an area threatened by Japanese attack.

In the light of the principles we announced in the *Hirabayashi* case, we are unable to conclude that it was beyond the war power of Congress and the Executive to exclude those of Japanese ancestry from the West Coast war area at the time they did. True, exclusion from the area in which one's home is located is a far greater deprivation than constant confinement to the home from 8 p.m. to 6 a.m. Nothing short of apprehension by the proper military authorities of the gravest imminent danger to the public safety can constitutionally justify either. But exclusion from a threatened area, no less than curfew, has a definite and close relationship to the prevention of espionage and sabotage. The military authorities, charged with the primary responsibility of defending our shores, concluded that curfew provided inadequate protection and ordered exclusion. They did so, as pointed out in our *Hirabayashi* opinion, in accordance with Congressional authority to the military to say who should, and who should not, remain in the threatened areas.

In this case, the petitioner challenges the assumptions upon which we rested our conclusions in the *Hirabayashi* case. He also urges that, by May, 1942, when Order No. 34 was promulgated, all danger of Japanese invasion of the West Coast had disappeared. After careful consideration of these contentions, we are compelled to reject them. . . .

Like curfew, exclusion of those of Japanese origin was deemed necessary because of the presence of an unascertained number of disloyal members of the group, most of whom we have no doubt were loyal to this country. It was because we could not reject the finding of the military authorities that it was impossible to bring about an immediate segregation of the disloyal from the loyal that we sustained the validity of the curfew order as applying to the whole group. In the instant case, temporary exclusion of the entire group was rested by the military on the same ground. The judgment that exclusion of the whole group was, for the same reason, a military imperative answers the contention that the exclusion was in the nature of group punishment based on antagonism to those of Japanese origin. That there were members of the group who retained loyalties to Japan has been confirmed by investigations made subsequent to the exclusion. Approximately five thousand American citizens of Japanese ancestry refused to swear unqualified allegiance to the United States and to renounce allegiance to the Japanese Emperor, and several thousand evacuees requested repatriation to Japan.

We uphold the exclusion order as of the time it was made and when the petitioner violated it. In doing so, we are not unmindful of the hardships imposed by it upon a large group of American citizens. But hardships are part of war, and war is an aggregation of hardships. All citizens alike, both in and out of uniform, feel the impact of war in greater or lesser measure. Citizenship has its responsibilities, as well as its privileges, and, in time of war, the burden is always heavier. Compulsory exclusion of large groups of citizens from their homes, except under circumstances of direst emergency and peril, is inconsistent with our basic governmental institutions. But when, under conditions of modern warfare, our shores are threatened by hostile forces, the power to protect must be commensurate with the threatened danger. . . .

It is said that we are dealing here with the case of imprisonment of a citizen in a concentration camp solely because of his ancestry, without evidence or inquiry concerning his loyalty and good disposition towards the United States. Our task would be simple, our duty clear, were this a case involving the imprisonment of a loyal citizen in a concentration camp because of racial prejudice. Regardless of the true nature of the assembly and relocation centers—and we deem it unjustifiable to call them concentration camps, with all the ugly connotations that term implies—we are dealing specifically with nothing but an exclusion order. To cast this case into outlines of racial prejudice, without reference to the real military dangers which were presented, merely confuses the issue. Korematsu was not excluded from the Military Area because of hostility to him or his race. He was excluded because we are at war with the Japanese Empire, because the properly constituted military authorities feared an invasion of our West Coast and felt constrained to take proper security measures, because they decided that the military urgency of the situation demanded that all citizens of Japanese ancestry be segregated from the West Coast temporarily, and, finally, because Congress, reposing its confidence in this time of war in our military leaders—as inevitably it must—determined that they should have the power to do just this. There was evidence of disloyalty on the part of some, the military authorities considered that the need for action was great, and time was short. We cannot—by availing ourselves of the calm perspective of hindsight—now say that, at that time, these actions were unjustified.

Affirmed.

Brown v. Board of Education of Topeka (1954)

> *This landmark case struck down the "separate but equal"*
> *doctrine established in* Plessy. *Specifically, the Supreme*
> *Court ruled that racial segregation could not continue in*
> *public schools under the Fourteenth Amendment's Equal*
> *Protection Clause. The impacts of this decision were also*
> *more far-reaching: segregation in other areas controlled*
> *by government, like public transportation, was barred.*

MR. CHIEF JUSTICE WARREN delivered the opinion
of the Court.

These cases come to us from the States of Kansas, South
Carolina, Virginia, and Delaware. They are premised on different facts and different local conditions, but a common
legal question justifies their consideration together in this
consolidated opinion.

In each of the cases, minors of the Negro race, through
their legal representatives, seek the aid of the courts in obtaining admission to the public schools of their community
on a nonsegregated basis. In each instance, they had been denied admission to schools attended by white children under
laws requiring or permitting segregation according to race.

This segregation was alleged to deprive the plaintiffs of the equal protection of the laws under the Fourteenth Amendment. . . .

The plaintiffs contend that segregated public schools are not "equal" and cannot be made "equal," and that hence they are deprived of the equal protection of the laws. Because of the obvious importance of the question presented, the Court took jurisdiction. . . .

Reargument was largely devoted to the circumstances surrounding the adoption of the Fourteenth Amendment in 1868. It covered exhaustively consideration of the Amendment in Congress, ratification by the states, then-existing practices in racial segregation, and the views of proponents and opponents of the Amendment. This discussion and our own investigation convince us that, although these sources cast some light, it is not enough to resolve the problem with which we are faced. At best, they are inconclusive. The most avid proponents of the post-War Amendments undoubtedly intended them to remove all legal distinctions among "all persons born or naturalized in the United States." Their opponents, just as certainly, were antagonistic to both the letter and the spirit of the Amendments and wished them to have the most limited effect. What others in Congress and the state legislatures had in mind cannot be determined with any degree of certainty.

An additional reason for the inconclusive nature of the Amendment's history with respect to segregated schools is the status of public education at that time. In the South, the movement toward free common schools, supported by general taxation, had not yet taken hold. Education of white children was largely in the hands of private groups. Education of Negroes was almost nonexistent, and practically all of the race were illiterate. In fact, any education of Negroes was forbidden by law in some states. Today, in contrast, many Negroes have achieved outstanding success in the arts and sciences, as well as in the business and professional world. It is true that public school education at the time of the Amendment had advanced further in the North, but the effect of the Amendment on Northern States was generally ignored in the congressional debates. Even in the North, the conditions of public education did not approximate those existing today. The curriculum was usually rudimentary; ungraded schools were common in rural areas; the school term was but three months a year in many states, and compulsory school attendance was virtually unknown. As a consequence, it is not surprising that there should be so little in the history of the Fourteenth Amendment relating to its intended effect on public education.

In the first cases in this Court construing the Fourteenth Amendment, decided shortly after its adoption, the Court interpreted it as proscribing all state-imposed discriminations against the Negro race. The doctrine of "separate but equal" did not make its appearance in this Court until 1896 in the case of *Plessy v. Ferguson*, involving not education but transportation. American courts have since labored with the doctrine for over half a century. . . .

In the instant cases, that question is directly presented. Here, unlike *Sweatt v. Painter*, there are findings below that the Negro and white schools involved have been equalized, or are being equalized, with respect to buildings, curricula, qualifications and salaries of teachers, and other "tangible" factors. Our decision, therefore, cannot turn on merely a comparison of these tangible factors in the Negro and white schools involved in each of the cases. We must look instead to the effect of segregation itself on public education.

In approaching this problem, we cannot turn the clock

back to 1868, when the Amendment was adopted, or even to 1896, when *Plessy v. Ferguson* was written. We must consider public education in the light of its full development and its present place in American life throughout the Nation. Only in this way can it be determined if segregation in public schools deprives these plaintiffs of the equal protection of the laws.

Today, education is perhaps the most important function of state and local governments. Compulsory school attendance laws and the great expenditures for education both demonstrate our recognition of the importance of education to our democratic society. It is required in the performance of our most basic public responsibilities, even service in the armed forces. It is the very foundation of good citizenship. Today it is a principal instrument in awakening the child to cultural values, in preparing him for later professional training, and in helping him to adjust normally to his environment. In these days, it is doubtful that any child may reasonably be expected to succeed in life if he is denied the opportunity of an education. Such an opportunity, where the state has undertaken to provide it, is a right which must be made available to all on equal terms.

We come then to the question presented: does segregation of children in public schools solely on the basis of race, even though the physical facilities and other "tangible" factors may be equal, deprive the children of the minority group of equal educational opportunities? We believe that it does. . . .

Such considerations apply with added force to children in grade and high schools. To separate them from others of similar age and qualifications solely because of their race generates a feeling of inferiority as to their status in the community that may affect their hearts and minds in a way unlikely ever to be undone. . . .

We conclude that, in the field of public education, the doctrine of "separate but equal" has no place. Separate educational facilities are inherently unequal. Therefore, we hold that the plaintiffs and others similarly situated for whom the actions have been brought are, by reason of the segregation complained of, deprived of the equal protection of the laws guaranteed by the Fourteenth Amendment. . . .

Because these are class actions, because of the wide applicability of this decision, and because of the great variety of local conditions, the formulation of decrees in these cases presents problems of considerable complexity. On reargument, the consideration of appropriate relief was necessarily subordinated to the primary question—the constitutionality of segregation in public education. We have now announced that such segregation is a denial of the equal protection of the laws. . . .

It is so ordered.

Cooper v. Aaron
(1958)

> *Following its decision in* Brown v. Board of Education, *the Supreme Court denied Arkansas's school board the right to delay desegregating its schools for thirty months. The case is also notable as it contained language suggesting that the Supreme Court not only has the power of judicial review, but that it has the final say about the American Constitution, a comment that has received criticism given the Court's deeply flawed Equal Protection rulings only a few years earlier.*

Opinion of the Court by THE CHIEF JUSTICE, MR. JUSTICE BLACK, MR. JUSTICE FRANKFURTER, MR. JUSTICE DOUGLAS, MR. JUSTICE BURTON, MR. JUSTICE CLARK, MR. JUSTICE HARLAN, MR. JUSTICE BRENNAN, and MR. JUSTICE WHITTAKER.

As this case reaches us, it raises questions of the highest importance to the maintenance of our federal system of government. It necessarily involves a claim by the Governor and Legislature of a State that there is no duty on state officials to obey federal court orders resting on this Court's considered interpretation of the United States Constitution. Specifically, it involves actions by the Governor and Legislature of Arkansas upon the premise that they are not bound by our holding in *Brown v. Board of Education.* . . . We are urged to uphold a suspension of the Little Rock School Board's plan to do away with segregated public schools in Little Rock until state laws and efforts to upset and nullify our holding in *Brown v. Board of Education* have been further challenged and tested in the courts. We reject these contentions. . . .

The following are the facts and circumstances so far as necessary to show how the legal questions are presented.

On May 17, 1954, this Court decided that enforced racial segregation in the public schools of a State is a denial of the equal protection of the laws enjoined by the Fourteenth Amendment. . . .

. . . It was made plain that delay in any guise in order to deny the constitutional rights of Negro children could not be countenanced, and that only a prompt start, diligently and earnestly pursued, to eliminate racial segregation from the public schools could constitute good faith compliance. State authorities were thus duty bound to devote every effort toward initiating desegregation and bringing about the elimination of racial discrimination in the public school system.

On May 20, 1954, three days after the first *Brown* opinion, the Little Rock District School Board adopted, and on May 23, 1954, made public, a statement of policy entitled "Supreme Court Decision—Segregation in Public Schools." In this statement, the Board recognized that

> "It is our responsibility to comply with Federal Constitutional Requirements, and we intend to do so when

the Supreme Court of the United States outlines the method to be followed."

Thereafter, the Board undertook studies of the administrative problems confronting the transition to a desegregated public school system at Little Rock. . . .

While the School Board was thus going forward with its preparation for desegregating the Little Rock school system, other state authorities, in contrast, were actively pursuing a program designed to perpetuate in Arkansas the system of racial segregation which this Court had held violated the Fourteenth Amendment. . . .

The School Board and the Superintendent of Schools nevertheless continued with preparations to carry out the first stage of the desegregation program. Nine Negro children were scheduled for admission in September, 1957, to Central High School, which has more than two thousand students. Various administrative measures, designed to assure the smooth transition of this first stage of desegregation, were undertaken. . . .

We come now to the aspect of the proceedings presently before us. On February 20, 1958, the School Board and the Superintendent of Schools filed a petition in the District Court seeking a postponement of their program for desegregation. Their position, in essence, was that, because of extreme public hostility, which they stated had been engendered largely by the official attitudes and actions of the Governor and the Legislature, the maintenance of a sound educational program at Central High School, with the Negro students in attendance, would be impossible. The Board therefore proposed that the Negro students already admitted to the school be withdrawn and sent to segregated schools, and that all further steps to carry out the Board's desegregation program be postponed for a period later suggested by the Board to be two and one-half years. . . .

In affirming the judgment of the Court of Appeals which reversed the District Court, we have accepted without reservation the position of the School Board, the Superintendent of Schools, and their counsel that they displayed entire good faith in the conduct of these proceedings and in dealing with the unfortunate and distressing sequence of events which has been outlined. We likewise have accepted the findings of the District Court as to the conditions at Central High School during the 1957–1958 school year, and also the findings that the educational progress of all the students, white and colored, of that school has suffered, and will continue to suffer if the conditions which prevailed last year are permitted to continue.

The significance of these findings, however, is to be considered in light of the fact, indisputably revealed by the record before us, that the conditions they depict are directly traceable to the actions of legislators and executive officials of the State of Arkansas, taken in their official capacities, which reflect their own determination to resist this Court's decision in the *Brown* case and which have brought about violent resistance to that decision in Arkansas. . . .

One may well sympathize with the position of the Board in the face of the frustrating conditions which have confronted it, but, regardless of the Board's good faith, the actions of the other state agencies responsible for those conditions compel us to reject the Board's legal position. . . .

The constitutional rights of respondents are not to be sacrificed or yielded to the violence and disorder which have followed upon the actions of the Governor and Legislature. . . .

Thus, law and order are not here to be preserved by depriving the Negro children of their constitutional rights. The record before us clearly establishes that the growth of the Board's difficulties to a magnitude beyond its unaided power to control is the product of state action. Those difficulties, as counsel for the Board forthrightly conceded on the oral argument in this Court, can also be brought under control by state action.

The controlling legal principles are plain. The command of the Fourteenth Amendment is that no "State" shall deny to any person within its jurisdiction the equal protection of the laws. . . .

What has been said, in the light of the facts developed, is enough to dispose of the case. However, we should answer the premise of the actions of the Governor and Legislature that they are not bound by our holding in the *Brown* case. It is necessary only to recall some basic constitutional propositions which are settled doctrine.

Article VI of the Constitution makes the Constitution the "supreme Law of the Land." In 1803, Chief Justice Marshall, speaking for a unanimous Court, referring to the Constitution as "the fundamental and paramount law of the nation," declared in the notable case of *Marbury v. Madison*, that "It is emphatically the province and duty of the judicial department to say what the law is." This decision declared the basic principle that the federal judiciary is supreme in the exposition of the law of the Constitution, and that principle has ever since been respected by this Court and the Country as a permanent and indispensable feature of our constitutional system. It follows that the interpretation of the Fourteenth Amendment enunciated by this Court in the *Brown* case is the supreme law of the land, and Art. VI of the Constitution makes it of binding effect on the States "any Thing in the Constitution or Laws of any State to the Contrary notwithstanding." Every state legislator and executive and judicial officer is solemnly committed by oath taken pursuant to Art. VI, cl. 3 "to support this Constitution." . . .

No state legislator or executive or judicial officer can war against the Constitution without violating his undertaking to support it. . . .

. . . The Constitution created a government dedicated to equal justice under law. The Fourteenth Amendment embodied and emphasized that ideal. State support of segregated schools through any arrangement, management, funds, or property cannot be squared with the Amendment's command that no State shall deny to any person within its jurisdiction the equal protection of the laws. The right of a student not to be segregated on racial grounds in schools so maintained is indeed so fundamental and pervasive that it is embraced in the concept of due process of law. The basic decision in *Brown* was unanimously reached by this Court only after the case had been briefed and twice argued and the issues had been given the most serious consideration. Since the first *Brown* opinion, three new Justices have come to the Court. They are at one with the Justices still on the Court who participated in that basic decision as to its correctness, and that decision is now unanimously reaffirmed. The principles announced in that decision and the obedience of the States to them, according to the command of the Constitution, are indispensable for the protection of the freedoms guaranteed by our fundamental charter for all of us. Our constitutional ideal of equal justice under law is thus made a living truth.

Loving v. Virginia
(1967)

A landmark civil rights decision, this case culminated in the Supreme Court ruling that laws prohibiting inter-racial marriages violated the Fourteenth Amendment.

MR. CHIEF JUSTICE WARREN delivered the opinion of the Court.

This case presents a constitutional question never addressed by this Court: whether a statutory scheme adopted by the State of Virginia to prevent marriages between persons solely on the basis of racial classifications violates the Equal Protection and Due Process Clauses of the Fourteenth Amendment. For reasons which seem to us to reflect the central meaning of those constitutional commands, we conclude that these statutes cannot stand consistently with the Fourteenth Amendment.

In June, 1958, two residents of Virginia, Mildred Jeter, a Negro woman, and Richard Loving, a white man, were married in the District of Columbia pursuant to its laws. Shortly after their marriage, the Lovings returned to Virginia and established their marital abode in Caroline County. At the October Term, 1958, of the Circuit Court of Caroline County, a grand jury issued an indictment charging the Lovings with violating Virginia's ban on interracial marriages. On January 6, 1959, the Lovings pleaded guilty to the charge, and were sentenced to one year in jail; however, the trial judge suspended the sentence for a period of 25 years on the condition that the Lovings leave the State and not return to Virginia together for 25 years. . . .

After their convictions, the Lovings took up residence in the District of Columbia. On November 6, 1963, they filed a motion in the state trial court to vacate the judgment and set aside the sentence on the ground that the statutes which they had violated were repugnant to the Fourteenth Amendment. . . .

The two statutes under which appellants were convicted and sentenced are part of a comprehensive statutory scheme aimed at prohibiting and punishing interracial marriages. . . .

Virginia is now one of 16 States which prohibit and punish marriages on the basis of racial classifications. Penalties for miscegenation arose as an incident to slavery, and have been common in Virginia since the colonial period. . . .

I

While the state court is no doubt correct in asserting that marriage is a social relation subject to the State's police power, *Maynard v. Hill* (1888), the State does not contend in its argument before this Court that its powers to regulate marriage are unlimited notwithstanding the commands of the Fourteenth Amendment. . . . Instead, the State argues that the meaning of the Equal Protection Clause, as illuminated by the statements of the Framers, is only that state penal laws containing an interracial element as part of the definition of the offense must apply equally to whites and Negroes in the sense that members of each race are punished to the same degree. Thus, the State contends that, because its miscegenation statutes punish equally both the white and the Negro participants in an interracial marriage, these statutes, despite their reliance on racial classifications, do not constitute an invidious discrimination based upon race. The second argument advanced by the State assumes the validity of its equal application theory. The argument is that, if the Equal Protection Clause does not outlaw miscegenation statutes because of their reliance on racial classifications, the question of constitutionality would thus become whether there was any rational basis for a State to treat interracial marriages differently from other marriages. On this question, the State argues, the scientific evidence is substantially in doubt and, consequently, this Court should defer to the wisdom of the state legislature in adopting its policy of discouraging interracial marriages.

Because we reject the notion that the mere "equal application" of a statute containing racial classifications is enough to remove the classifications from the Fourteenth Amendment's proscription of all invidious racial discriminations, we do not accept the State's contention that these statutes should be upheld if there is any possible basis for concluding that they serve a rational purpose. . . .

The State argues that statements in the Thirty-ninth Congress about the time of the passage of the Fourteenth Amendment indicate that the Framers did not intend the Amendment to make unconstitutional state miscegenation laws. . . . While these statements have some relevance to the intention of Congress in submitting the Fourteenth Amendment, it must be

understood that they pertained to the passage of specific statutes, and not to the broader, organic purpose of a constitutional amendment. . . .

We have rejected the proposition that the debates in the
Thirty-ninth Congress or in the state legislatures which ratified the Fourteenth Amendment supported the theory advanced by the State, that the requirement of equal protection
of the laws is satisfied by penal laws defining offenses based
on racial classifications so long as white and Negro participants in the offense were similarly punished. . . .

There can be no question but that Virginia's miscegenation statutes rest solely upon distinctions drawn according to
race. The statutes proscribe generally accepted conduct if engaged in by members of different races. . . .

There is patently no legitimate overriding purpose independent of invidious racial discrimination which justifies this
classification. The fact that Virginia prohibits only interracial
marriages involving white persons demonstrates that the racial classifications must stand on their own justification, as
measures designed to maintain White Supremacy. We have
consistently denied the constitutionality of measures which
restrict the rights of citizens on account of race. There can be
no doubt that restricting the freedom to marry solely because
of racial classifications violates the central meaning of the
Equal Protection Clause.

II

These statutes also deprive the Lovings of liberty without due
process of law in violation of the Due Process Clause of
the Fourteenth Amendment. The freedom to marry has long

been recognized as one of the vital personal rights essential to the orderly pursuit of happiness by free men.

Marriage is one of the "basic civil rights of man," fundamental to our very existence and survival. To deny this fundamental freedom on so unsupportable a basis as the racial classifications embodied in these statutes, classifications so directly subversive of the principle of equality at the heart of the Fourteenth Amendment, is surely to deprive all the State's citizens of liberty without due process of law. The Fourteenth Amendment requires that the freedom of choice to marry not be restricted by invidious racial discriminations. Under our Constitution, the freedom to marry, or not marry, a person of another race resides with the individual, and cannot be infringed by the State.

These convictions must be reversed.

It is so ordered.

Plyler v. Doe
(1982)

> *In this landmark case, the Supreme Court ruled that the Fourteenth Amendment's Equal Protection Clause and other rights contained in the Constitution applied to undocumented children in the United States. In doing so, the Court allowed undocumented children to receive an education in public schools across the country and further expanded access to rights contained in the Constitution.*

JUSTICE BRENNAN delivered the opinion of the Court.

The question presented by these cases is whether, consistent with the Equal Protection Clause of the Fourteenth Amendment, Texas may deny to undocumented school-age children the free public education that it provides to children who are citizens of the United States or legally admitted aliens.

I

Since the late 19th century, the United States has restricted immigration into this country. Unsanctioned entry into the

United States is a crime, and those who have entered unlawfully are subject to deportation. But despite the existence of these legal restrictions, a substantial number of persons have succeeded in unlawfully entering the United States, and now live within various States, including the State of Texas.

In May, 1975, the Texas Legislature revised its education laws to withhold from local school districts any state funds for the education of children who were not "legally admitted" into the United States. The 1975 revision also authorized local school districts to deny enrollment in their public schools to children not "legally admitted" to the country. These cases involve constitutional challenges to those provisions. . . .

II

The Fourteenth Amendment provides that

> "[n]o State shall . . . deprive any person of life, liberty, or property, without due process of law; nor deny to any person within its jurisdiction the equal protection of the laws."

Appellants argue at the outset that undocumented aliens, because of their immigration status, are not "persons within the jurisdiction" of the State of Texas, and that they therefore have no right to the equal protection of Texas law. We reject this argument. Whatever his status under the immigration laws, an alien is surely a "person" in any ordinary sense of that term. Aliens, even aliens whose presence in this country is unlawful, have long been recognized as "persons" guaranteed due process of law by the Fifth and Fourteenth Amendments. Indeed, we have clearly held that the Fifth Amendment protects aliens whose presence in this country is unlawful from invidious discrimination by the Federal Government.

Appellants seek to distinguish our prior cases, emphasizing that the Equal Protection Clause directs a State to afford its protection to persons *within its jurisdiction*, while the Due Process Clauses of the Fifth and Fourteenth Amendments contain no such assertedly limiting phrase. In appellants' view, persons who have entered the United States illegally are not "within the jurisdiction" of a State even if they are present within a State's boundaries and subject to its laws. Neither our cases nor the logic of the Fourteenth Amendment support that constricting construction of the phrase "within its jurisdiction." . . .

In concluding that "all persons within the territory of the United States," including aliens unlawfully present, may invoke the Fifth and Sixth Amendments to challenge actions of the Federal Government, we reasoned from the understanding that the Fourteenth Amendment was designed to afford its protection to all within the boundaries of a State. . . .

. . . To permit a State to employ the phrase "within its jurisdiction" in order to identify subclasses of persons whom it would define as beyond its jurisdiction, thereby relieving itself of the obligation to assure that its laws are designed and applied equally to those persons, would undermine the principal purpose for which the Equal Protection Clause was incorporated in the Fourteenth Amendment. The Equal Protection Clause was intended to work nothing less than the abolition of all caste-based and invidious class-based legislation. That objective is fundamentally at odds with the power the State asserts here to classify persons subject to its laws as nonetheless excepted from its protection. . . .

Use of the phrase "within its jurisdiction" thus does not detract from, but rather confirms, the understanding that the protection of the Fourteenth Amendment extends to anyone, citizen or stranger, who *is* subject to the laws of a State, and reaches into every corner of a State's territory. That a person's initial entry into a State, or into the United States, was unlawful, and that he may for that reason be expelled, cannot negate the simple fact of his presence within the State's territorial perimeter. Given such presence, he is subject to the full range of obligations imposed by the State's civil and criminal laws. And until he leaves the jurisdiction—either voluntarily, or involuntarily in accordance with the Constitution and laws of the United States—he is entitled to the equal protection of the laws that a State may choose to establish.

Our conclusion that the illegal aliens who are plaintiffs in these cases may claim the benefit of the Fourteenth Amendment's guarantee of equal protection only begins the inquiry. The more difficult question is whether the Equal Protection Clause has been violated by the refusal of the State of Texas to reimburse local school boards for the education of children who cannot demonstrate that their presence within the United States is lawful, or by the imposition by those school boards of the burden of tuition on those children. It is to this question that we now turn.

III

The Equal Protection Clause directs that "all persons similarly circumstanced shall be treated alike." . . . In applying the Equal Protection Clause to most forms of state action, we thus seek only the assurance that the classification at issue bears some fair relationship to a legitimate public purpose.

But we would not be faithful to our obligations under the Fourteenth Amendment if we applied so deferential a standard to every classification. The Equal Protection Clause was intended as a restriction on state legislative action inconsistent with elemental constitutional premises. Thus, we have treated as presumptively invidious those classifications that disadvantage a "suspect class," or that impinge upon the exercise of a "fundamental right." With respect to such classifications, it is appropriate to enforce the mandate of equal protection by requiring the State to demonstrate that its classification has been precisely tailored to serve a compelling governmental interest. . . .

A

Sheer incapability or lax enforcement of the laws barring entry into this country, coupled with the failure to establish an effective bar to the employment of undocumented aliens, has resulted in the creation of a substantial "shadow population" of illegal migrants—numbering in the millions—within our borders. This situation raises the specter of a permanent caste of undocumented resident aliens, encouraged by some to remain here as a source of cheap labor, but nevertheless denied the benefits that our society makes available to citizens and lawful residents. The existence of such an underclass presents most difficult problems for a Nation that prides itself on adherence to principles of equality under law.

The children who are plaintiffs in these cases are special members of this underclass. Persuasive arguments support the view that a State may withhold its beneficence from those whose very presence within the United States is the product of their own unlawful conduct. These arguments do not apply with the same force to classifications imposing disabilities on the minor children of such illegal entrants. At the least, those who elect to enter our territory by stealth and in violation of our law should be prepared to bear the consequences, including, but not limited to, deportation. But the children of those illegal entrants are not comparably situated. Their "parents have the ability to conform their conduct to societal norms," and presumably the ability to remove themselves from the State's jurisdiction; but the children who are plaintiffs in these cases "can affect neither their parents' conduct nor their own status." . . . Even if the State found it expedient to control the conduct of adults by acting against their children, legislation directing the onus of a parent's misconduct against his children does not comport with fundamental conceptions of justice. . . .

Of course, undocumented status is not irrelevant to any proper legislative goal. Nor is undocumented status an absolutely immutable characteristic, since it is the product of conscious, indeed unlawful, action. But § 21.031 is directed against children, and imposes its discriminatory burden on the basis of a legal characteristic over which children can have little control. It is thus difficult to conceive of a rational justification for penalizing these children for their presence within the United States. . . .

Public education is not a "right" granted to individuals by the Constitution. But neither is it merely some governmental "benefit" indistinguishable from other forms of social welfare legislation. Both the importance of education in maintaining our basic institutions and the lasting impact of its deprivation on the life of the child mark the distinction. . . . We have recognized "the public schools as a most vital civic institution for the preservation of a democratic system of government," and as the primary vehicle for transmitting "the values on which our society rests." . . .

In addition, education provides the basic tools by which individuals might lead economically productive lives to the benefit of us all. In sum, education has a fundamental role in maintaining the fabric of our society. We cannot ignore the significant social costs borne by our Nation when select groups are denied the means to absorb the values and skills upon which our social order rests.

In addition to the pivotal role of education in sustaining our political and cultural heritage, denial of education to some isolated group of children poses an affront to one of the goals of the Equal Protection Clause: the abolition of governmental barriers presenting unreasonable obstacles to advancement on the basis of individual merit. Paradoxically, by depriving the children of any disfavored group of an education, we foreclose the means by which that group might raise the level of esteem in which it is held by the majority. But more directly, "education prepares individuals to be self-reliant and self-sufficient participants in society." Illiteracy is an enduring disability. The inability to read and write will handicap the individual deprived of a basic education each and every day of his life. The inestimable toll of that deprivation on the social, economic, intellectual, and psychological well-being of the individual, and the obstacle it poses to individual achievement, make it most difficult to reconcile the cost or the principle of a status-based denial of basic education with the framework of equality embodied in the Equal Protection Clause. . . .

V

. . . First, appellants appear to suggest that the State may seek to protect itself from an influx of illegal immigrants. While a State might have an interest in mitigating the potentially harsh economic effects of sudden shifts in population, § 21.031

hardly offers an effective method of dealing with an urgent demographic or economic problem. There is no evidence in the record suggesting that illegal entrants impose any significant burden on the State's economy. To the contrary, the available evidence suggests that illegal aliens underutilize public services, while contributing their labor to the local economy and tax money to the state. The dominant incentive for illegal entry into the State of Texas is the availability of employment; few if any illegal immigrants come to this country, or presumably to the State of Texas, in order to avail themselves of a free education. Thus, even making the doubtful assumption that the net impact of illegal aliens on the economy of the State is negative, we think it clear that "[c]harging tuition to undocumented children constitutes a ludicrously ineffectual attempt to stem the tide of illegal immigration," at least when compared with the alternative of prohibiting the employment of illegal aliens. . . .

Finally, appellants suggest that undocumented children are appropriately singled out because their unlawful presence within the United States renders them less likely than other children to remain within the boundaries of the State, and to put their education to productive social or political use within the State. Even assuming that such an interest is legitimate, it is an interest that is most difficult to quantify. The State has no assurance that any child, citizen or not, will employ the education provided by the State within the confines of the State's borders. . . .

VI

If the State is to deny a discrete group of innocent children the free public education that it offers to other children residing within its borders, that denial must be justified by a showing that it furthers some substantial state interest. No such showing was made here. Accordingly, the judgment of the Court of Appeals in each of these cases is

Affirmed.

Gratz v. Bollinger (2003)

> *The Supreme Court ruled in this landmark case that the University of Michigan's use of race in a point system for undergraduate admissions violated the Fourteenth Amendment's Equal Protection Clause.*

CHIEF JUSTICE REHNQUIST delivered the opinion of the Court.

We granted certiorari in this case to decide whether "the University of Michigan's use of racial preferences in undergraduate admissions violate[s] the Equal Protection Clause of the Fourteenth Amendment, Title VI of the Civil Rights Act of 1964, or 42 U.S.C. § 1981."

Because we find that the manner in which the University considers the race of applicants in its undergraduate admissions guidelines violates these constitutional and statutory provisions, we reverse that portion of the District Court's decision upholding the guidelines.

I

A

Petitioners Jennifer Gratz and Patrick Hamacher both applied for admission to the University of Michigan's (University) College of Literature, Science, and the Arts (LSA) as residents of the State of Michigan. Both petitioners are Caucasian. Gratz, who applied for admission for the fall of 1995, was notified in January of that year that a final decision regarding her admission had been delayed until April. This delay was based upon the University's determination that, although Gratz was "'well qualified,'" she was "'less competitive than the students who ha[d] been admitted on first review.'" Gratz was notified in April that the LSA was unable to offer her admission. She enrolled in the University of Michigan at Dearborn, from which she graduated in the spring of 1999.

Hamacher applied for admission to the LSA for the fall of 1997. A final decision as to his application was also postponed because, though his "'academic credentials [were] in the qualified range, they [were] not at the level needed for first review admission.'" Hamacher's application was subsequently denied in April 1997, and he enrolled at Michigan State University.

In October 1997, Gratz and Hamacher filed a lawsuit in the United States District Court for the Eastern District of Michigan against the University, the LSA, James Duderstadt, and Lee Bollinger. Petitioners' complaint was a class-action suit alleging "violations and threatened violations of the rights of the plaintiffs and the class they represent to equal protection of the laws under the Fourteenth Amendment . . . , and for racial discrimination in violation of 42 U.S.C. §§ 1981, 1983 and 2000d *et seq.*" . . .

B

The University has changed its admissions guidelines a number of times during the period relevant to this litigation, and we summarize the most significant of these changes briefly. The University's Office of Undergraduate Admissions (OUA) oversees the LSA admissions process. In order to promote consistency in the review of the large number of applications received, the OUA uses written guidelines for each academic year. Admissions counselors make admissions decisions in accordance with these guidelines.

OUA considers a number of factors in making admissions decisions, including high school grades, standardized test scores, high school quality, curriculum strength, geography, alumni relationships, and leadership. OUA also considers race. During all periods relevant to this litigation, the University has considered African-Americans, Hispanics, and Native Americans to be "underrepresented minorities," and it is undisputed that the University admits "virtually every qualified . . . applicant" from these groups.

During 1995 and 1996, OUA counselors evaluated applications according to grade point average combined with what were referred to as the "SCUGA" factors. These factors included the quality of an applicant's high school (S), the strength of an applicant's high school curriculum (C), an applicant's unusual circumstances (U), an applicant's geographical residence (G), and an applicant's alumni relationships (A). After these scores were combined to produce an applicant's "GPA 2" score, the reviewing admissions counselors referenced a set of "Guidelines" tables, which listed GPA 2 ranges on the vertical axis, and American College Test/ Scholastic Aptitude Test (ACT/SAT) scores on the horizontal axis. Each table was divided into cells that included one or more courses of action to be taken, including admit, reject, delay for additional information, or postpone for reconsideration.

In both years, applicants with the same GPA 2 score and ACT/SAT score were subject to different admissions outcomes based upon their racial or ethnic status. For example, as a Caucasian in-state applicant, Gratz's GPA 2 score and ACT score placed her within a cell calling for a postponed decision on her application. An in-state or out-of-state minority applicant with Gratz's scores would have fallen within a cell calling for admission.

In 1997, the University modified its admissions procedure. Specifically, the formula for calculating an applicant's GPA 2 score was restructured to include additional point values under the "U" category in the SCUGA factors. Under this new system, applicants could receive points for underrepresented minority status, socioeconomic disadvantage, or attendance at a high school with a predominantly underrepresented minority population, or underrepresentation in the unit to which the student was applying (for example, men who sought to pursue a career in nursing). Under the 1997 procedures, Hamacher's GPA 2 score and ACT score placed him in a cell on the in-state applicant table calling for postponement of a final admissions decision. An underrepresented minority applicant placed in the same cell would generally have been admitted.

Beginning with the 1998 academic year, the OUA dispensed with the Guidelines tables and the SCUGA point system in favor of a "selection index," on which an applicant could score a maximum of 150 points. This index was divided linearly into ranges generally calling for admissions dispositions as follows: 100–150 (admit); 95–99 (admit or postpone); 90–94 (postpone or admit); 75–89 (delay or postpone); 74 and below (delay or reject).

Each application received points based on high school grade point average, standardized test scores, academic quality of an applicant's high school, strength or weakness of high school curriculum, in-state residency, alumni relationship, personal essay, and personal achievement or leadership. Of particular significance here, under a "miscellaneous" category, an applicant was entitled to 20 points based upon his or her membership in an underrepresented racial or ethnic minority group. . . .

In all application years from 1995 to 1998, the guidelines provided that qualified applicants from underrepresented minority groups be admitted as soon as possible in light of the University's belief that such applicants were more likely to enroll if promptly notified of their admission. . . .

During 1999 and 2000, the OUA used the selection index, under which every applicant from an underrepresented racial or ethnic minority group was awarded 20 points. Starting in 1999, however, the University established an Admissions Review Committee (ARC), to provide an additional level of consideration for some applications. . . .

II

As they have throughout the course of this litigation, petitioners contend that the University's consideration of race in its undergraduate admissions decisions violates § 1 of the Equal Protection Clause of the Fourteenth Amendment, Title VI, and 42 U.S.C. § 1981. . . .

B

. . . It is by now well established that "all racial classifications reviewable under the Equal Protection Clause must be strictly scrutinized." This "'standard of review . . . is not dependent on the race of those burdened or benefited by a particular classification.'" Thus, "any person, of whatever race, has the right to demand that any governmental actor subject to the Constitution justify any racial classification subjecting that person to unequal treatment under the strictest of judicial scrutiny."

To withstand our strict scrutiny analysis, respondents must demonstrate that the University's use of race in its current admissions program employs "narrowly tailored measures that further compelling governmental interests." . . . We find that the University's policy, which automatically distributes 20 points, or one-fifth of the points needed to guarantee admission, to every single "underrepresented minority" applicant solely because of race, is not narrowly tailored to achieve the interest in educational diversity that respondents claim justifies their program.

In *Bakke*, Justice Powell reiterated that "[p]referring members of anyone group for no reason other than race or ethnic origin is discrimination for its own sake." He then explained, however, that in his view it would be permissible for a university to employ an admissions program in which "race or ethnic background may be deemed a 'plus' in a particular applicant's file." . . . Such a system, in Justice Powell's view, would be "flexible enough to consider all pertinent elements of diversity in light of the particular qualifications of each applicant."

Justice Powell's opinion in *Bakke* emphasized the importance of considering each particular applicant as an individual, assessing all of the qualities that individual possesses, and in turn, evaluating that individual's ability to contribute to the unique setting of higher education. The admissions program Justice Powell described, however, did not contemplate that any single characteristic automatically ensured a specific and identifiable contribution to a university's diversity. . . . Instead, under the approach Justice Powell described, each characteristic of a particular applicant was to be considered in assessing the applicant's entire application.

The current LSA policy does not provide such individualized consideration. The LSA's policy automatically distributes 20 points to every single applicant from an "underrepresented minority" group, as defined by the University. The only consideration that accompanies this distribution of points is a factual review of an application to determine whether an individual is a member of one of these minority groups. . . .

. . . Instead of considering how the differing backgrounds, experiences, and characteristics of students A, B, and C might benefit the University, admissions counselors reviewing LSA applications would simply award both A and B 20 points because their applications indicate that they are African-American, and student C would receive up to 5 points for his "extraordinary talent." . . .

We conclude, therefore, that because the University's use of race in its current freshman admissions policy is not narrowly tailored to achieve respondents' asserted compelling interest in diversity, the admissions policy violates the Equal Protection Clause of the Fourteenth Amendment. We further find that the admissions policy also violates Title VI and

42 U.S.C. § 1981. Accordingly, we reverse that portion of the District Court's decision granting respondents summary judgment with respect to liability and remand the case for proceedings consistent with this opinion.

It is so ordered.

Grutter v. Bollinger (2003)

While the Supreme Court struck down the undergraduate system of admission at the University of Michigan as conflicting with the Fourteenth Amendment's Equal Protection Clause, in this case it upheld a "narrowly tailored" system of affirmative action that included diversity as a factor in admission but avoided quotas or overly rigid methods for considering race as an advantage for a candidate.

JUSTICE O'CONNOR delivered the opinion of the Court. This case requires us to decide whether the use of race as a factor in student admissions by the University of Michigan Law School (Law School) is unlawful.

. . . The Law School ranks among the Nation's top law schools.

It receives more than 3,500 applications each year for a class of around 350 students. Seeking to "admit a group of students who individually and collectively are among the most capable," the Law School looks for individuals with "substantial promise for success in law school" and "a strong likelihood of succeeding in the practice of law and contributing in diverse ways to the well-being of others." More broadly, the Law School seeks "a mix of students with varying backgrounds and experiences who will respect and learn from each other." In 1992, the dean of the Law School charged a faculty committee with crafting a written admissions policy to implement these goals. In particular, the Law School sought to ensure that its efforts to achieve student body diversity complied with this Court's most recent ruling on the use of race in university admissions.

Upon the unanimous adoption of the committee's report by the Law School faculty, it became the Law School's official admissions policy.

The hallmark of that policy is its focus on academic ability coupled with a flexible assessment of applicants' talents, experiences, and potential "to contribute to the learning of those around them." The policy requires admissions officials to evaluate each applicant based on all the information available in the file, including a personal statement, letters of recommendation, and an essay describing the ways in which the applicant will contribute to the life and diversity of the Law School. In reviewing an applicant's file, admissions officials must consider the applicant's undergraduate grade point average (GPA) and Law School Admissions Test (LSAT) score because they are important (if imperfect) predictors of academic success in law school. The policy stresses that "no applicant should be admitted unless we expect that applicant to do well enough to graduate with no serious academic problems."

The policy makes clear, however, that even the highest possible score does not guarantee admission to the Law School. Nor does a low score automatically disqualify an applicant. Rather, the policy requires admissions officials to look beyond grades and test scores to other criteria that are important to the Law School's educational objectives. So-called "'soft' variables" such as "the enthusiasm of recommenders, the quality of the undergraduate institution, the quality of the applicant's essay, and the areas and difficulty of undergraduate course selection" are all brought to bear in assessing an "applicant's likely contributions to the intellectual and social life of the institution."

The policy aspires to "achieve that diversity which has the potential to enrich everyone's education and thus make a law school class stronger than the sum of its parts."

The policy does not restrict the types of diversity contributions eligible for "substantial weight" in the admissions process, but instead recognizes "many possible bases for diversity admissions." The policy does, however, reaffirm the Law School's longstanding commitment to "one particular type of diversity," that is, "racial and ethnic diversity with special reference to the inclusion of students from groups which have been historically discriminated against, like African-Americans, Hispanics and Native Americans, who without this commitment might not be represented in our student body in meaningful numbers." By enrolling a "'critical mass' of [underrepresented] minority students," the Law School seeks to "ensur[e] their ability to make unique contributions to the character of the Law School."

The policy does not define diversity "solely in terms of racial and ethnic status." Nor is the policy "insensitive to the competition among all students for admission to the [L]aw [S]chool." Rather, the policy seeks to guide admissions officers in "producing classes both diverse and academically outstanding, classes made up of students who promise to continue the tradition of outstanding contribution by Michigan Graduates to the legal profession." . . .

Petitioner Barbara Grutter is a white Michigan resident

who applied to the Law School in 1996 with a 3.8 grade point average and 161 LSAT score. The Law School initially placed petitioner on a waiting list, but subsequently rejected her application. In December 1997, petitioner filed suit in the United States District Court for the Eastern District of Michigan against the Law School, the Regents of the University of Michigan, Lee Bollinger (Dean of the Law School from 1987 to 1994, and President of the University of Michigan from 1996 to 2002), Jeffrey Lehman (Dean of the Law School), and Dennis Shields (Director of Admissions at the Law School from 1991 until 1998). Petitioner alleged that respondents discriminated against her on the basis of race in violation of the Fourteenth Amendment. . . .

Petitioner further alleged that her application was rejected because the Law School uses race as a "predominant" factor, giving applicants who belong to certain minority groups "a significantly greater chance of admission than students with similar credentials from disfavored racial groups." Petitioner also alleged that respondents "had no compelling interest to justify their use of race in the admissions process." Petitioner requested compensatory and punitive damages, an order requiring the Law School to offer her admission, and an injunction prohibiting the Law School from continuing to discriminate on the basis of race. Petitioner clearly has standing to bring this lawsuit. . . .

During the 15-day bench trial, the parties introduced extensive evidence concerning the Law School's use of race in the admissions process. Dennis Shields, Director of Admissions when petitioner applied to the Law School, testified that he did not direct his staff to admit a particular percentage or number of minority students, but rather to consider an applicant's race along with all other factors. Shields testified that at the height of the admissions season, he would frequently consult the so-called "daily reports" that kept track of the racial and ethnic composition of the class (along with other information such as residency status and gender). This was done, Shields testified, to ensure that a critical mass of underrepresented minority students would be reached so as to realize the educational benefits of a diverse student body. Shields stressed, however, that he did not seek to admit any particular number or percentage of underrepresented minority students.

Erica Munzel, who succeeded Shields as Director of Admissions, testified that "'critical mass'" means "'meaningful numbers'" or "'meaningful representation,'" which she understood to mean a number that encourages underrepresented minority students to participate in the classroom and not feel isolated. Munzel stated there is no number, percentage, or range of numbers or percentages that constitute critical mass. Munzel also asserted that she must consider the race of applicants because a critical mass of underrepresented minority students could not be enrolled if admissions decisions were based primarily on undergraduate GPAs and LSAT scores. . . .

In an attempt to quantify the extent to which the Law School actually considers race in making admissions decisions, the parties introduced voluminous evidence at trial. Relying on data obtained from the Law School, petitioner's expert, Dr. Kinley Larntz, generated and analyzed "admissions grids" for the years in question (1995–2000). These grids show the number of applicants and the number of admittees for all combinations of GPAs and LSAT scores. Dr. Larntz made "'cell-by-cell'" comparisons between applicants of different races to determine whether a statistically significant relationship existed between race and admission rates. He concluded that membership in certain minority groups "'is an extremely strong factor in the decision for acceptance,'" and that applicants from these minority groups "'are given an extremely large allowance for admission'" as compared to applicants who are members of nonfavored groups. Dr. Larntz conceded, however, that race is not the predominant factor in the Law School's admissions calculus.

Dr. Stephen Raudenbush, the Law School's expert, focused on the predicted effect of eliminating race as a factor in the Law School's admission process. In Dr. Raudenbush's view, a race-blind admissions system would have a "'very dramatic,'" negative effect on underrepresented minority admissions. He testified that in 2000, 35 percent of underrepresented minority applicants were admitted. Dr. Raudenbush predicted that if race were not considered, only 10 percent of those applicants would have been admitted. Under this scenario, underrepresented minority students would have comprised 4 percent of the entering class in 2000 instead of the actual figure of 14.5 percent. . . .

The Equal Protection Clause provides that no State shall "deny to any person within its jurisdiction the equal protection of the laws." Because the Fourteenth Amendment "protect[s] *persons*, not *groups*," all "governmental action based on race—a *group* classification long recognized as in most circumstances irrelevant and therefore prohibited—should be subjected to detailed judicial inquiry to ensure that the *personal* right to equal protection of the laws has not been infringed." We are a "free people whose institutions are founded upon the doctrine of equality." It follows from that principle that "government may treat people differently because of their race only for the most compelling reasons." . . .

With these principles in mind, we turn to the question whether the Law School's use of race is justified by a compelling state interest. Before this Court, as they have throughout this litigation, respondents assert only one justification for their use of race in the admissions process: obtaining "the educational benefits that flow from a diverse student body." In other words, the Law School asks us to recognize, in the context of higher education, a compelling state interest in student body diversity.

We first wish to dispel the notion that the Law School's argument has been foreclosed, either expressly or implicitly, by our affirmative-action cases decided since *Bakke*. It is true that some language in those opinions might be read to suggest that remedying past discrimination is the only permissible justification for race-based governmental action. But we have never held that the only governmental use of race that can survive strict scrutiny is remedying past discrimination. Nor, since *Bakke*, have we directly addressed the use of race in the context of public higher education. Today, we hold that the Law School has a compelling interest in attaining a diverse student body.

The Law School's educational judgment that such diversity is essential to its educational mission is one to which we defer. The Law School's assessment that diversity will, in fact, yield educational benefits is substantiated by respondents and their *amici*. Our scrutiny of the interest asserted by the Law School is no less strict for taking into account complex educational judgments in an area that lies primarily within the expertise of the university. Our holding today is in keeping with our tradition of giving a degree of deference to a university's academic decisions, within constitutionally prescribed limits.

We have long recognized that, given the important purpose of public education and the expansive freedoms of speech and thought associated with the university environment, universities occupy a special niche in our constitutional tradition. In announcing the principle of student body diversity as a compelling state interest, Justice Powell invoked our cases recognizing a constitutional dimension, grounded in the First Amendment, of educational autonomy: "The freedom of a university to make its own judgments as to education includes the selection of its student body." From this premise, Justice Powell reasoned that by claiming "the right to select those students who will contribute the most to the 'robust exchange of ideas,'" a university "seek[s] to achieve a goal that is of paramount importance in the fulfillment of its mission." Our conclusion that the Law School has a compelling interest in a diverse student body is informed by our view that attaining a diverse student body is at the heart of the Law School's proper institutional mission, and that "good faith" on the part of a university is "presumed" absent "a showing to the contrary."

As part of its goal of "assembling a class that is both exceptionally academically qualified and broadly diverse," the Law School seeks to "enroll a 'critical mass' of minority students." The Law School's interest is not simply "to assure within its student body some specified percentage of a particular group merely because of its race or ethnic origin." That would amount to outright racial balancing, which is patently unconstitutional. Rather, the Law School's concept of critical mass is defined by reference to the educational benefits that diversity is designed to produce.

These benefits are substantial. As the District Court emphasized, the Law School's admissions policy promotes "cross-racial understanding," helps to break down racial stereotypes, and "enables [students] to better understand persons of different races." These benefits are "important and laudable," because "classroom discussion is livelier, more spirited, and simply more enlightening and interesting" when the students have "the greatest possible variety of backgrounds."

The Law School's claim of a compelling interest is further bolstered by its *amici*, who point to the educational benefits that flow from student body diversity. In addition to the expert studies and reports entered into evidence at trial, numerous studies show that student body diversity promotes learning outcomes, and "better prepares students for an increasingly diverse workforce and society, and better prepares them as professionals."

These benefits are not theoretical but real, as major American businesses have made clear that the skills needed in today's increasingly global marketplace can only be developed through exposure to widely diverse people, cultures, ideas, and viewpoints. What is more, high-ranking retired officers and civilian leaders of the United States military assert that, "[b]ased on [their] decades of experience," a "highly qualified, racially diverse officer corps . . . is essential to the military's ability to fulfill its principle mission to provide national security." The primary sources for the Nation's officer corps are the service academies and the Reserve Officers Training Corps (ROTC), the latter comprising students already admitted to participating colleges and universities. At present, "the military cannot achieve an officer corps that is *both* highly qualified *and* racially diverse unless the service academies and the ROTC used limited race-conscious recruiting and admissions policies." To fulfill its mission, the military "must be selective in admissions for training and education for the officer corps, *and* it must train and educate a highly qualified, racially diverse officer corps in a racially diverse setting." We agree that "[i]t requires only a small step from this analysis to conclude that our country's other most selective institutions must remain both diverse and selective."

We have repeatedly acknowledged the overriding importance of preparing students for work and citizenship, describing education as pivotal to "sustaining our political and cultural heritage" with a fundamental role in maintaining the fabric of society. This Court has long recognized that "education . . . is the very foundation of good citizenship." For this reason, the diffusion of knowledge and opportunity through public institutions of higher education must be accessible to all individuals regardless of race or ethnicity. The United States, as *amicus curiae*, affirms that "[e]nsuring that public institutions are open and available to all segments of American society, including people of all races and ethnicities, represents a paramount government objective." And, "[n]owhere is the importance of such openness more acute than in the context of higher education." Effective participation by members of all racial and ethnic groups in the civic life of our Nation is essential if the dream of one Nation, indivisible, is to be realized.

Moreover, universities, and in particular, law schools, represent the training ground for a large number of our Nation's leaders. Individuals with law degrees occupy roughly half the state governorships, more than half the seats in the United States Senate, and more than a third of the seats in the United States House of Representatives. The pattern is even more striking when it comes to highly selective law schools. A handful of these schools accounts for 25 of the 100 United States Senators, 74 United States Courts of Appeals judges, and nearly 200 of the more than 600 United States District Court judges.

In order to cultivate a set of leaders with legitimacy in the eyes of the citizenry, it is necessary that the path to leadership be visibly open to talented and qualified individuals of every race and ethnicity. All members of our heterogeneous society must have confidence in the openness and integrity of the educational institutions that provide this training. As we have recognized, law schools "cannot be effective in isolation from the individuals and institutions with which the law interacts." Access to legal education (and thus the legal profession) must be inclusive of talented and qualified individuals of every race and ethnicity, so that all members of our heterogeneous society may participate in the educational institutions that provide the training and education necessary to succeed in America.

The Law School does not premise its need for critical mass on "any belief that minority students always (or even consistently) express some characteristic minority viewpoint on any issue." To the contrary, diminishing the force of such stereotypes is both a crucial part of the Law School's mission, and one that it cannot accomplish with only token numbers of minority students. Just as growing up in a particular region or having particular professional experiences is likely to affect an individual's views, so too is one's own, unique experience of being a racial minority in a society, like our own, in which race unfortunately still matters. The Law School has determined, based on its experience and expertise, that a "critical mass" of underrepresented minorities is necessary to further its compelling interest in securing the educational benefits of a diverse student body. . . .

Even in the limited circumstance when drawing racial distinctions is permissible to further a compelling state interest, government is still "constrained in how it may pursue that end: [T]he means chosen to accomplish the [government's] asserted purpose must be specifically and narrowly framed to accomplish that purpose." The purpose of the narrow tailoring requirement is to ensure that "the means chosen 'fit' . . . th[e] compelling goal so closely that there is little or no possibility that the motive for the classification was illegitimate racial prejudice or stereotype."

Since *Bakke*, we have had no occasion to define the contours of the narrow-tailoring inquiry with respect to race-conscious university admissions programs. That inquiry must be calibrated to fit the distinct issues raised by the use of race to achieve student body diversity in public higher education. Contrary to JUSTICE KENNEDY's assertions, we do not "abando[n] strict scrutiny." Rather, as we have already explained, we adhere to *Adarand*'s teaching that the very purpose of strict scrutiny is to take such "relevant differences into account."

To be narrowly tailored, a race-conscious admissions program cannot use a quota system—it cannot "insulat[e] each category of applicants with certain desired qualifications from competition with all other applicants." Instead, a university may consider race or ethnicity only as a "'plus' in a particular applicant's file," without "insulat[ing] the individual from comparison with all other candidates for the available seats." In other words, an admissions program must be "flexible enough to consider all pertinent elements of diversity in light of the particular qualifications of each applicant, and to place them on the same footing for consideration, although not necessarily according them the same weight."

We find that the Law School's admissions program bears the hallmarks of a narrowly tailored plan. As Justice Powell made clear in *Bakke*, truly individualized consideration demands that race be used in a flexible, nonmechanical way. It follows from this mandate that universities cannot establish quotas for members of certain racial groups or put members of those groups on separate admissions tracks. Nor can universities insulate applicants who belong to certain racial or ethnic groups from the competition for admission. Universities can, however, consider race or ethnicity more flexibly as a "plus" factor in the context of individualized consideration of each and every applicant.

We are satisfied that the Law School's admissions program, like the Harvard plan described by Justice Powell, does not operate as a quota. Properly understood, a "quota" is a program in which a certain fixed number or proportion of opportunities are "reserved exclusively for certain minority groups." Quotas "'impose a fixed number or percentage which must be attained, or which cannot be exceeded,'" and "insulate the individual from comparison with all other candidates for the available seats." In contrast, "a permissible goal . . . require[s] only a good-faith effort . . . to come within a range demarcated by the goal itself," and permits consideration of race as a "plus" factor in any given case while still ensuring that each candidate "compete[s] with all other qualified applicants."

Justice Powell's distinction between the medical school's rigid 16-seat quota and Harvard's flexible use of race as a "plus" factor is instructive. Harvard certainly had minimum *goals* for minority enrollment, even if it had no specific number firmly in mind. What is more, Justice Powell flatly rejected the argument that Harvard's program was "the functional equivalent of a quota" merely because it had some "'plus'" for race, or gave greater "weight" to race than to some other factors, in order to achieve student body diversity.

The Law School's goal of attaining a critical mass of underrepresented minority students does not transform its program into a quota. As the Harvard plan described by Justice Powell recognized, there is of course "some relationship between numbers and achieving the benefits to be derived from a diverse student body, and between numbers and providing a reasonable environment for those students admitted."

"[S]ome attention to numbers," without more, does not transform a flexible admissions system into a rigid quota. Nor, as
JUSTICE KENNEDY posits, does the Law School's consultation of the "daily reports," which keep track of the racial
and ethnic composition of the class (as well as of residency
and gender), "sugges[t] there was no further attempt at individual review save for race itself" during the final stages of
the admissions process. To the contrary, the Law School's
admissions officers testified without contradiction that they
never gave race any more or less weight based on the information contained in these reports. Moreover, as JUSTICE
KENNEDY concedes, the number of African-American,
Latino, and Native-American students in each class at the
Law School varied from 13.5 to 20.1 percent, a range inconsistent with a quota.

THE CHIEF JUSTICE believes that the Law School's
policy conceals an attempt to achieve racial balancing, and
cites admissions data to contend that the Law School dis-
criminates among different groups within the critical mass.
But, as the THE CHIEF JUSTICE concedes, the number
of underrepresented minority students who ultimately enroll
in the Law School differs substantially from their representation in the applicant pool and varies considerably for each
group from year to year.

That a race-conscious admissions program does not operate as a quota does not, by itself, satisfy the requirement of
individualized consideration. When using race as a "plus"
factor in university admissions, a university's admissions program must remain flexible enough to ensure that each applicant is evaluated as an individual and not in a way that makes
an applicant's race or ethnicity the defining feature of his or
her application. The importance of this individualized con-

sideration in the context of a race-conscious admissions program is paramount.

Here, the Law School engages in a highly individualized, holistic review of each applicant's file, giving serious consideration to all the ways an applicant might contribute to a diverse educational environment. The Law School affords this individualized consideration to applicants of all races. There is no policy, either *de jure* or *de facto*, of automatic acceptance or rejection based on any single "soft" variable. Unlike the program at issue in *Gratz v. Bollinger*, the Law School awards no mechanical, predetermined diversity "bonuses" based on race or ethnicity. Like the Harvard plan, the Law School's admissions policy "is flexible enough to consider all pertinent elements of diversity in light of the particular qualifications of each applicant, and to place them on the same footing for consideration, although not necessarily according them the same weight." . . .

The Law School does not, however, limit in any way the broad range of qualities and experiences that may be considered valuable contributions to student body diversity. To the contrary, the 1992 policy makes clear "[t]here are many possible bases for diversity admissions," and provides examples of admittees who have lived or traveled widely abroad, are fluent in several languages, have overcome personal adversity and family hardship, have exceptional records of extensive community service, and have had successful careers in other fields. The Law School seriously considers each "applicant's promise of making a notable contribution to the class by way of a particular strength, attainment, or characteristic—e.g., an unusual intellectual achievement, employment experience, nonacademic performance, or personal background." All applicants have the opportunity to highlight their own potential diversity contributions through the submission of a personal statement, letters of recommendation, and an essay describing the ways in which the applicant will contribute to the life and diversity of the Law School.

What is more, the Law School actually gives substantial weight to diversity factors besides race. The Law School frequently accepts nonminority applicants with grades and test scores lower than underrepresented minority applicants (and other nonminority applicants) who are rejected. This shows that the Law School seriously weighs many other diversity factors besides race that can make a real and dispositive difference for nonminority applicants as well. By this flexible approach, the Law School sufficiently takes into account, in practice as well as in theory, a wide variety of characteristics besides race and ethnicity that contribute to a diverse student body. JUSTICE KENNEDY speculates that "race is likely outcome determinative for many members of minority groups" who do not fall within the upper range of LSAT scores and grades. But the same could be said of the Harvard plan discussed approvingly by Justice Powell in *Bakke*, and indeed of any plan that uses race as one of many factors.

Petitioner and the United States argue that the Law School's plan is not narrowly tailored because race-neutral means exist to obtain the educational benefits of student body diversity that the Law School seeks. We disagree. Narrow tailoring does not require exhaustion of every conceivable race-neutral alternative. Nor does it require a university to choose between maintaining a reputation for excellence or fulfilling a commitment to provide educational opportunities to members of all racial groups. Narrow tailoring does, however, require serious, good faith consideration of workable race-neutral alternatives that will achieve the diversity the university seeks. . . .

The Law School's current admissions program considers race as one factor among many, in an effort to assemble a student body that is diverse in ways broader than race. Because a lottery would make that kind of nuanced judgment impossible, it would effectively sacrifice all other educational values, not to mention every other kind of diversity. So too with the suggestion that the Law School simply lower admissions standards for all students, a drastic remedy that would require the Law School to become a much different institution and sacrifice a vital component of its educational mission. The United States advocates "percentage plans," recently adopted by public undergraduate institutions in Texas, Florida, and California to guarantee admission to all students above a certain class-rank threshold in every high school in the State. The United States does not, however, explain how such plans could work for graduate and professional schools. Moreover, even assuming such plans are race-neutral, they may preclude the university from conducting the individualized assessments necessary to assemble a student body that is not just racially diverse, but diverse along all the qualities valued by the university. We are satisfied that the Law School adequately considered race-neutral alternatives currently capable of producing a critical mass without forcing the Law School to abandon the academic selectivity that is the cornerstone of its educational mission.

We acknowledge that "there are serious problems of justice connected with the idea of preference itself." Narrow tailoring, therefore, requires that a race-conscious admissions program not unduly harm members of any racial group. Even remedial race-based governmental action generally "remains subject to continuing oversight to assure that it will work the least harm possible to other innocent persons competing for the benefit." To be narrowly tailored, a race-conscious admissions program must not "unduly burden individuals who are not members of the favored racial and ethnic groups."

We are satisfied that the Law School's admissions program does not. Because the Law School considers "all pertinent elements of diversity," it can (and does) select nonminority applicants who have greater potential to enhance student body diversity over underrepresented minority applicants. As Justice Powell recognized in *Bakke*, so long as a race-conscious admissions program uses race as a "plus" factor in the context of individualized consideration, a rejected applicant

> "will not have been foreclosed from all consideration for that seat simply because he was not the right color or had the wrong surname. . . . His qualifications would have been weighed fairly and competitively, and he would have no basis to complain of unequal treatment under the Fourteenth Amendment."

We agree that, in the context of its individualized inquiry into the possible diversity contributions of all applicants, the Law School's race-conscious admissions program does not unduly harm nonminority applicants.

We are mindful, however, that "[a] core purpose of the Fourteenth Amendment was to do away with all governmentally imposed discrimination based on race." Accordingly, race-conscious admissions policies must be limited in time. This requirement reflects that racial classifications, however compelling their goals, are potentially so dangerous that they may be employed no more broadly than the interest demands. Enshrining a permanent justification for racial preferences would offend this fundamental equal protection principle. We see no reason to exempt race-conscious admissions programs from the requirement that all governmental use of race must have a logical end point. The Law School, too, concedes that all "race-conscious programs must have reasonable durational limits."

In the context of higher education, the durational requirement can be met by sunset provisions in race-conscious admissions policies and periodic reviews to determine whether racial preferences are still necessary to achieve student body diversity. Universities in California, Florida, and Washington State, where racial preferences in admissions are prohibited by state law, are currently engaged in experimenting with a wide variety of alternative approaches. Universities in other States can and should draw on the most promising aspects of these race-neutral alternatives as they develop.

The requirement that all race-conscious admissions programs have a termination point "assure[s] all citizens that the deviation from the norm of equal treatment of all racial and ethnic groups is a temporary matter, a measure taken in the service of the goal of equality itself."

We take the Law School at its word that it would "like nothing better than to find a race-neutral admissions formula" and will terminate its race-conscious admissions program as soon as practicable. It has been 25 years since Justice Powell first approved the use of race to further an interest in student body diversity in the context of public higher education. Since that time, the number of minority applicants with high grades and test scores has indeed increased. We expect that 25 years from now, the use of racial preferences will no longer be necessary to further the interest approved today.

In summary, the Equal Protection Clause does not prohibit the Law School's narrowly tailored use of race in admissions decisions to further a compelling interest in obtaining the educational benefits that flow from a diverse student body. Consequently, petitioner's statutory claims based on Title VI and 42 U.S.C. § 1981 also fail. The judgment of the Court of Appeals for the Sixth Circuit, accordingly, is affirmed.

It is so ordered.

Part III

FREEDOM OF SPEECH

———— ☆ ————

This part examines the Supreme Court's willingness to sacrifice free speech for national security in the early twentieth century, as well as its course correction later in the century to prioritize speech even when a president cited national security concerns. Pay attention to this evolution as you read the included cases.

Schenck v. United States (1919)

In this case, the Supreme Court considered whether a pamphlet urging draft resistance during World War I was protected free speech. The Court, in a famous opinion by Justice Holmes, ruled that it was not protected because the speech posed a "clear and present danger" to the security of the United States. For much of the twentieth century, the Court would use the rationale of "clear and present danger" to limit free speech, in particular when it came from those on the left of the political spectrum, including communists and anarchists.

MR. JUSTICE HOLMES delivered the opinion of the court.

This is an indictment in three counts. The first charges a conspiracy to violate the Espionage Act of June 15, 1917, by causing and attempting to cause insubordination . . . in the military and naval forces of the United States, and to obstruct the recruiting and enlistment service of the United States, when the United States was at war with the German Empire . . . the defendants willfully conspired to have printed and circulated to men who had been called and accepted for military service under the Act of May 18, 1917, a document set forth and alleged to be calculated to cause such insubordination and obstruction. . . . The second count alleges a conspiracy to commit an offence against the United States, . . . to use the mails for the transmission of matter declared to be nonmailable by Title XII, § 2 of the Act of June 15, 1917, . . . with an averment of the same overt acts. The third count charges an unlawful use of the mails for the transmission of the same matter and otherwise as above. The defendants were found guilty on all the counts. They set up the First Amendment to the Constitution forbidding Congress to make any law abridging the freedom of speech, or of the press, and bringing the case here on that ground have argued some other points also of which we must dispose. . . .

The document in question, upon its first printed side, recited the first section of the Thirteenth Amendment, said that the idea embodied in it was violated by the Conscription Act, and that a conscript is little better than a convict. In impassioned language, it intimated that conscription was despotism in its worst form, and a monstrous wrong against humanity in the interest of Wall Street's chosen few. . . .

It described the arguments on the other side as coming from cunning politicians and a mercenary capitalist press, and even silent consent to the conscription law as helping to support an infamous conspiracy. It denied the power to send our citizens away to foreign shores to shoot up the people of other lands, and added that words could not express the condemnation such cold-blooded ruthlessness deserves, . . . winding up, "You must do your share to maintain, support and uphold the rights of the people of this country." Of course, the document would not have been sent unless it had been intended to have some effect, and we do not see what effect it could be expected to have upon persons subject to the draft except to influence them to obstruct the carrying of it out. The defendants do not deny that the jury might find against them on this point.

But it is said, suppose that that was the tendency of this circular, it is protected by the First Amendment to the Constitution. . . . We admit that, in many places and in ordinary times, the defendants, in saying all that was said in the circular, would have been within their constitutional rights. But the character of every act depends upon the circumstances in which it is done. The most stringent protection of free speech would not protect a man in falsely shouting fire in a theatre and causing a panic. It does not even protect a man from an injunction against uttering words that may have all the effect of force. The question in every case is whether the words used are used in such circumstances and are of such a nature as to create a clear and present danger that they will bring about the substantive evils that Congress has a right to prevent. It is a question of proximity and degree. When a nation is at war, many things that might be said in time of peace are such a hindrance to its effort that their utterance will not be endured so long as men fight, and that no Court could regard them as protected by any constitutional right. . . .

Judgments affirmed.

Brandenburg v. Ohio
(1969)

In 1969 the Supreme Court reconsidered the "clear and present danger" doctrine, ushering in a more stringent standard that would only allow advocacy of "lawless action," including revolution and political violence, to be limited if it posed an "imminent" threat and was intended to do so. This case shielded a speaker at a Ku Klux Klan rally from prosecution on the grounds that his speech was protected.

PER CURIAM

The appellant, a leader of a Ku Klux Klan group, was convicted under the Ohio Criminal Syndicalism statute for "advocat[ing] . . . the duty, necessity, or propriety of crime, sabotage, violence, or unlawful methods of terrorism as a means of accomplishing industrial or political reform" and for "voluntarily assembl[ing] with any society, group, or assemblage of persons formed to teach or advocate the doctrines of criminal syndicalism."

He was fined $1,000 and sentenced to one to 10 years' imprisonment. The appellant challenged the constitutionality of the criminal syndicalism statute under the First and Fourteenth Amendments to the United States Constitution, but the intermediate appellate court of Ohio affirmed his conviction without opinion. The Supreme Court of Ohio dismissed his appeal *sua sponte* "for the reason that no substantial constitutional question exists herein." It did not file an opinion or explain its conclusions. Appeal was taken to this Court, and we noted probable jurisdiction. We reverse.

The record shows that a man, identified at trial as the appellant, telephoned an announcer-reporter on the staff of a Cincinnati television station and invited him to come to a Ku Klux Klan "rally" to be held at a farm in Hamilton County. With the cooperation of the organizers, the reporter and a cameraman attended the meeting and filmed the events. Portions of the films were later broadcast on the local station and on a national network.

The prosecution's case rested on the films and on testimony identifying the appellant as the person who communicated with the reporter and who spoke at the rally. The State also introduced into evidence several articles appearing in the film, including a pistol, a rifle, a shotgun, ammunition, a Bible, and a red hood worn by the speaker in the films.

One film showed 12 hooded figures, some of whom carried firearms. They were gathered around a large wooden cross, which they burned. No one was present other than the participants and the newsmen who made the film. Most of the words uttered during the scene were incomprehensible when the film was projected, but scattered phrases could be understood that were derogatory of Negroes and, in one instance, of Jews. Another scene on the same film showed the appellant, in Klan regalia, making a speech. The speech, in full, was as follows:

"This is an organizers' meeting. We have had quite a few members here today which are—we have hundreds, hundreds of members throughout the State of Ohio. I can quote from a newspaper clipping from the Columbus, Ohio, Dispatch, five weeks ago Sunday morning. The Klan has more members in the State of Ohio than does any other organization. We're not a revengent organization, but if our President, our Congress, our Supreme Court, continues to suppress the white, Caucasian race, it's possible that there might have to be some revengeance taken.

"We are marching on Congress July the Fourth, four hundred thousand strong. From there, we are dividing into two groups, one group to march on St. Augustine, Florida, the other group to march into Mississippi. Thank you."

The second film showed six hooded figures one of whom, later identified as the appellant, repeated a speech very similar to that recorded on the first film. The reference to the possibility of "revengeance" was omitted, and one sentence was added: "Personally, I believe the nigger should be returned to Africa, the Jew returned to Israel." Though some of the figures in the films carried weapons, the speaker did not.

The Ohio Criminal Syndicalism Statute was enacted in 1919. From 1917 to 1920, identical or quite similar laws were adopted by 20 States and two territories. In 1927, this Court sustained the constitutionality of California's Criminal Syndicalism Act, the text of which is quite similar to that of the laws of Ohio. The Court upheld the statute on the ground that, without more, "advocating" violent means to effect political and economic change involves such danger to the security of the State that the State may outlaw it. But *Whitney* has been thoroughly discredited by later decisions. These later decisions have fashioned the principle that the constitutional guarantees of free speech and free press do not permit a State to forbid or proscribe advocacy of the use of force or of law violation except where such advocacy is directed to inciting or producing imminent lawless action and is likely to incite or produce such action. As we said in *Noto v. United States* (1961), "the mere abstract teaching . . . of the moral propriety or even moral necessity for a resort to force and violence is not the same as preparing a group for violent action and steeling it to such action."

A statute which fails to draw this distinction impermissibly intrudes upon the freedoms guaranteed by the First and Fourteenth Amendments. It sweeps within its condemnation speech which our Constitution has immunized from governmental control.

Measured by this test, Ohio's Criminal Syndicalism Act cannot be sustained. The Act punishes persons who "advocate or teach the duty, necessity, or propriety" of violence "as a means of accomplishing industrial or political reform"; or who publish or circulate or display any book or paper containing such advocacy; or who "justify" the commission of violent acts "with intent to exemplify, spread or advocate the propriety of the doctrines of criminal syndicalism"; or who "voluntarily assemble" with a group formed "to teach or advocate the doctrines of criminal syndicalism." Neither the indictment nor the trial judge's instructions to the jury in any way refined the statute's bald definition of the crime in terms of mere advocacy not distinguished from incitement to imminent lawless action.

Accordingly, we are here confronted with a statute which, by its own words and as applied, purports to punish mere advocacy and to forbid, on pain of criminal punishment, assembly with others merely to advocate the described type of action. Such a statute falls within the condemnation of the First and Fourteenth Amendments. The contrary teaching of *Whitney v. California* cannot be supported, and that decision is therefore overruled.

Reversed.

MR. JUSTICE BLACK, concurring.

I agree with the views expressed by MR. JUSTICE DOUGLAS in his concurring opinion in this case that the "clear and present danger" doctrine should have no place in the interpretation of the First Amendment. I join the Court's opinion, which, as I understand it, simply cites *Dennis v. United States*, (1951), but does not indicate any agreement on the Court's part with the "clear and present danger" doctrine on which *Dennis* purported to rely.

MR. JUSTICE DOUGLAS, concurring.

While I join the opinion of the Court, I desire to enter a *caveat*.

The "clear and present danger" test was adumbrated by Mr. Justice Holmes in a case arising during World War I— a war "declared" by the Congress, not by the Chief Executive. The case was *Schenck v. United States*, where the defendant was charged with attempts to cause insubordination in the military and obstruction of enlistment. The pamphlets that were distributed urged resistance to the draft, denounced conscription, and impugned the motives of those backing the war effort. The First Amendment was tendered as a defense. Mr. Justice Holmes, in rejecting that defense, said:

"The question in every case is whether the words used are used in such circumstances and are of such a nature as to create a clear and present danger that they will bring about the substantive evils that Congress has a right to prevent. It is a question of proximity and degree."

Frohwerk v. United States, also authored by Mr. Justice Holmes, involved prosecution and punishment for publication of articles very critical of the war effort in World War I. *Schenck* was referred to as a conviction for obstructing security "by words of persuasion." And the conviction in *Frohwerk* was sustained because "the circulation of the paper was in quarters where a little breath would be enough to kindle a flame."

Debs v. United States was the third of the trilogy of the 1918 Term. Debs was convicted of speaking in opposition to the war where his "opposition was so expressed that its natural and intended effect would be to obstruct recruiting.

"If that was intended, and if, in all the circumstances, that would be its probable effect, it would not be protected by reason of its being part of a general program and expressions of a general and conscientious belief."

In the 1919 Term, the Court applied the *Schenck* doctrine to affirm the convictions of other dissidents in World War I. *Abrams v. United States* was one instance. Mr. Justice Holmes, with whom Mr. Justice Brandeis concurred, dissented. While adhering to *Schenck*, he did not think that, on the facts, a case for overriding the First Amendment had been made out:

"It is only the present danger of immediate evil or an intent to bring it about that warrants Congress in setting a limit to the expression of opinion where private rights are not concerned. Congress certainly cannot forbid all effort to change the mind of the country."

Another instance was *Schaefer v. United States*, in which Mr. Justice Brandeis, joined by Mr. Justice Holmes, dissented. A third was *Pierce v. United States*, in which, again, Mr. Justice Brandeis, joined by Mr. Justice Holmes, dissented.

Those, then, were the World War I cases that put the gloss of "clear and present danger" on the First Amendment. Whether the war power—the greatest leveler of them all—is adequate to sustain that doctrine is debatable.

The dissents in *Abrams*, *Schaefer*, and *Pierce* show how easily "clear and present danger" is manipulated to crush what Brandeis called "[t]he fundamental right of free men to strive for better conditions through new legislation and new institutions" by argument and discourse even in time of war. Though I doubt if the "clear and present danger" test is congenial to the First Amendment in time of a declared war, I am certain it is not reconcilable with the First Amendment in days of peace.

The Court quite properly overrules *Whitney v. California*, which involved advocacy of ideas which the majority of the Court deemed unsound and dangerous.

Mr. Justice Holmes, though never formally abandoning the "clear and present danger" test, moved closer to the First Amendment ideal when he said in dissent in *Gitlow v. New York*:

"Every idea is an incitement. It offers itself for belief, and, if believed, it is acted on unless some other belief outweighs it or some failure of energy stifles the movement at its birth. The only difference between the expression of an opinion and an incitement in the narrower sense is the speaker's enthusiasm for the result. Eloquence may set fire to reason. But whatever may be thought of the redundant discourse before us, it had no chance of starting a present conflagration. If, in the long run, the beliefs expressed in proletarian dictatorship are destined to be accepted by the dominant forces of the community, the only meaning of free speech is that they should be given their chance and have their way."

We have never been faithful to the philosophy of that dissent.

The Court, in *Herndon v. Lowry*, overturned a conviction for exercising First Amendment rights to incite insurrection because of lack of evidence of incitement. In *Bridges v. California*, we approved the "clear and present danger" test in an elaborate dictum that tightened it and confined it to a narrow category. But in *Dennis v. United States*, we opened wide the door, distorting the "clear and present danger" test beyond recognition.

In that case, the prosecution dubbed an agreement to teach the Marxist creed a "conspiracy." The case was submitted to a jury on a charge that the jury could not convict unless it found that the defendants "intended to overthrow the Government as speedily as circumstances would permit." The Court sustained convictions under that charge, construing it to mean a determination of "'whether the gravity of the evil,' discounted by its improbability, justifies such invasion of free speech as is necessary to avoid the danger."

Out of the "clear and present danger" test came other offspring. Advocacy and teaching of forcible overthrow of government as an abstract principle is immune from prosecution.

But an "active" member, who has a guilty knowledge and intent of the aim to overthrow the Government by violence, *Noto v. United States*, may be prosecuted. And the power to investigate, backed by the powerful sanction of contempt, includes the power to determine which of the two categories fits the particular witness. And so the investigator roams at will through all of the beliefs of the witness, ransacking his conscience and his innermost thoughts.

Judge Learned Hand, who wrote for the Court of Appeals in affirming the judgment in *Dennis*, coined the "not improbable" test, which this Court adopted and which Judge Hand preferred over the "clear and present danger" test. Indeed, in his book, *The Bill of Rights* (1958), in referring to Holmes' creation of the "clear and present danger" test, he said, "I cannot help thinking that, for once, Homer nodded."

My own view is quite different. I see no place in the regime of the First Amendment for any "clear and present danger" test, whether strict and tight, as some would make it, or free-wheeling, as the Court in *Dennis* rephrased it.

When one reads the opinions closely and sees when and how the "clear and present danger" test has been applied, great misgivings are aroused. First, the threats were often loud, but always puny, and made serious only by judges so wedded to the *status quo* that critical analysis made them nervous. Second, the test was so twisted and perverted in *Dennis* as to make the trial of those teachers of Marxism an all-out political trial which was part and parcel of the cold war that has eroded substantial parts of the First Amendment.

Action is often a method of expression, and within the protection of the First Amendment.

Suppose one tears up his own copy of the Constitution in eloquent protest to a decision of this Court. May he be indicted?

Suppose one rips his own Bible to shreds to celebrate his departure from one "faith" and his embrace of atheism. May he be indicted?

Last Term, the Court held in *United States v. O'Brien* that a registrant under Selective Service who burned his draft card in protest of the war in Vietnam could be prosecuted. The First Amendment was tendered as a defense and rejected, the Court saying:

> "The issuance of certificates indicating the registration and eligibility classification of individuals is a legitimate and substantial administrative aid in the functioning of this system. And legislation to insure the continuing availability of issued certificates serves a legitimate and substantial purpose in the system's administration."

But O'Brien was not prosecuted for not having his draft card available when asked for by a federal agent. He was indicted, tried, and convicted for burning the card. And this Court's affirmance of that conviction was not, with all respect, consistent with the First Amendment.

The act of praying often involves body posture and movement, as well as utterances. It is nonetheless protected by the Free Exercise Clause. Picketing, as we have said on numerous occasions, is "free speech plus." That means that it can be regulated when it comes to the "plus" or "action" side of the protest. It can be regulated as to the number of pickets and the place and hours because traffic and other community problems would otherwise suffer.

But none of these considerations is implicated in the symbolic protest of the Vietnam war in the burning of a draft card.

One's beliefs have long been thought to be sanctuaries which government could not invade. *Barenblatt* is one example of the ease with which that sanctuary can be violated. The lines drawn by the Court between the criminal act of being an "active" Communist and the innocent act of being a nominal or inactive Communist mark the difference only between deep and abiding belief and casual or uncertain belief. But I think that all matters of belief are beyond the reach of subpoenas or the probings of investigators. That is why the invasions of privacy made by investigating committees were notoriously unconstitutional. That is the deep-seated fault in the infamous loyalty security hearings which, since 1947, when President Truman launched them, have processed 20,000,000 men and women. Those hearings were primarily concerned with one's thoughts, ideas, beliefs, and convictions. They were the most blatant violations of the First Amendment we have ever known.

The line between what is permissible and not subject to control and what may be made impermissible and subject to regulation is the line between ideas and overt acts.

The example usually given by those who would punish speech is the case of one who falsely shouts fire in a crowded theatre.

This is, however, a classic case where speech is brigaded with action. They are indeed inseparable, and a prosecution can be launched for the overt acts actually caused. Apart from rare instances of that kind, speech is, I think, immune from prosecution. Certainly there is no constitutional line between advocacy of abstract ideas, as in *Yates*, and advocacy of political action, as in *Scales*. The quality of advocacy turns on the depth of the conviction, and government has no power to invade that sanctuary of belief and conscience.

Tinker v. Des Moines Independent Community School District (1969)

> *After a public school suspended students who wore black armbands to protest the country's involvement in the Vietnam War, the Supreme Court ruled that this decision violated the students' First Amendment right to the freedom of speech.*

MR. JUSTICE FORTAS delivered the opinion of the Court.

Petitioner John F. Tinker, 15 years old, and petitioner Christopher Eckhardt, 16 years old, attended high schools in Des Moines, Iowa. Petitioner Mary Beth Tinker, John's sister, was a 13-year-old student in junior high school.

In December, 1965, a group of adults and students in Des Moines held a meeting at the Eckhardt home. The group determined to publicize their objections to the hostilities in Vietnam and their support for a truce by wearing black armbands during the holiday season and by fasting on December 16 and New Year's Eve. Petitioners and their parents had previously engaged in similar activities, and they decided to participate in the program.

The principals of the Des Moines schools became aware

of the plan to wear armbands. On December 14, 1965, they met and adopted a policy that any student wearing an armband to school would be asked to remove it, and, if he refused, he would be suspended until he returned without the armband. . . .

On December 16, Mary Beth and Christopher wore black armbands to their schools. John Tinker wore his armband the next day. They were all sent home and suspended from school until they would come back without their armbands. They did not return to school until after the planned period for wearing armbands had expired—that is, until after New Year's Day.

This complaint was filed in the United States District Court by petitioners, through their fathers, under § 1983 of Title 42 of the United States Code. It prayed for an injunction restraining the respondent school officials and the respondent members of the board of directors of the school district from disciplining the petitioners, and it sought nominal damages. After an evidentiary hearing, the District Court dismissed the complaint. It upheld the constitutionality of the school authorities' action on the ground that it was reasonable in order to prevent disturbance of school discipline. . . .

On appeal, the Court of Appeals for the Eighth Circuit considered the case *en banc*. The court was equally divided, and the District Court's decision was accordingly affirmed without opinion. We granted certiorari.

I

The District Court recognized that the wearing of an armband for the purpose of expressing certain views is the type of symbolic act that is within the Free Speech Clause of the First Amendment. . . . As we shall discuss, the wearing of armbands in the circumstances of this case was entirely divorced from actually or potentially disruptive conduct by those participating in it. It was closely akin to "pure speech" which, we have repeatedly held, is entitled to comprehensive protection under the First Amendment.

First Amendment rights, applied in light of the special characteristics of the school environment, are available to teachers and students. It can hardly be argued that either students or teachers shed their constitutional rights to freedom of speech or expression at the schoolhouse gate. This has been the unmistakable holding of this Court for almost 50 years. . . .

On the other hand, the Court has repeatedly emphasized the need for affirming the comprehensive authority of the States and of school officials, consistent with fundamental constitutional safeguards, to prescribe and control conduct in the schools. Our problem lies in the area where students in the exercise of First Amendment rights collide with the rules of the school authorities.

II

The problem posed by the present case does not relate to regulation of the length of skirts or the type of clothing, to hair style, or deportment. It does not concern aggressive, disruptive action or even group demonstrations. Our problem involves direct, primary First Amendment rights akin to "pure speech."

The school officials banned and sought to punish petitioners for a silent, passive expression of opinion, unaccompanied by any disorder or disturbance on the part of petitioners. There is here no evidence whatever of petitioners' interference, actual or nascent, with the schools' work or of collision with the rights of other students to be secure and to be let alone. Accordingly, this case does not concern speech or action that intrudes upon the work of the schools or the rights of other students.

Only a few of the 18,000 students in the school system wore the black armbands. Only five students were suspended for wearing them. There is no indication that the work of the schools or any class was disrupted. Outside the classrooms, a few students made hostile remarks to the children wearing armbands, but there were no threats or acts of violence on school premises.

The District Court concluded that the action of the school authorities was reasonable because it was based upon their fear of a disturbance from the wearing of the armbands. But, in our system, undifferentiated fear or apprehension of disturbance is not enough to overcome the right to freedom of expression. . . .

In order for the State in the person of school officials to justify prohibition of a particular expression of opinion, it must be able to show that its action was caused by something more than a mere desire to avoid the discomfort and unpleasantness that always accompany an unpopular viewpoint. Certainly where there is no finding and no showing that engaging in the forbidden conduct would "materially and substantially interfere with the requirements of appropriate discipline in the operation of the school," the prohibition cannot be sustained.

In the present case, the District Court made no such finding, and our independent examination of the record fails to yield evidence that the school authorities had reason to anticipate that the wearing of the armbands would substantially interfere with the work of the school or impinge upon the rights of other students. Even an official memorandum prepared after the suspension that listed the reasons for the ban on wearing the armbands made no reference to the anticipation of such disruption.

On the contrary, the action of the school authorities appears to have been based upon an urgent wish to avoid the controversy which might result from the expression, even by the silent symbol of armbands, of opposition to this Nation's part in the conflagration in Vietnam. It is revealing, in this respect, that the meeting at which the school principals decided to issue the contested regulation was called in response to a student's statement to the journalism teacher in one of the schools that he wanted to write an article on Vietnam and have it published in the school paper. (The student was dissuaded.)

It is also relevant that the school authorities did not purport to prohibit the wearing of all symbols of political or controversial significance. The record shows that students in some of the schools wore buttons relating to national political campaigns, and some even wore the Iron Cross, traditionally a symbol of Nazism. The order prohibiting the wearing of armbands did not extend to these. Instead, a particular symbol—black armbands worn to exhibit opposition to this Nation's involvement in Vietnam—was singled out for prohibition. Clearly, the prohibition of expression of one particular opinion, at least without evidence that it is necessary to avoid material and substantial interference with schoolwork or discipline, is not constitutionally permissible.

In our system, state-operated schools may not be enclaves of totalitarianism. School officials do not possess absolute authority over their students. Students in school, as well as out of school, are "persons" under our Constitution. They are possessed of fundamental rights which the State must respect, just as they themselves must respect their obligations to the State. In our system, students may not be regarded as closed-circuit recipients of only that which the State chooses to communicate. They may not be confined to the expression of those sentiments that are officially approved. In the absence of a specific showing of constitutionally valid reasons to regulate their speech, students are entitled to freedom of expression of their views. . . .

. . . The principal use to which the schools are dedicated is to accommodate students during prescribed hours for the purpose of certain types of activities. Among those activities is personal intercommunication among the students. This is not only an inevitable part of the process of attending school; it is also an important part of the educational process. A student's rights, therefore, do not embrace merely the classroom hours. When he is in the cafeteria, or on the playing field, or on the campus during the authorized hours, he may express his opinions, even on controversial subjects like the conflict in Vietnam, if he does so without "materially and substantially interfer[ing] with the requirements of appropriate discipline in the operation of the school" and without colliding with the rights of others. But conduct by the student, in class or out of it, which for any reason—whether it stems from time, place, or type of behavior—materially disrupts classwork or involves substantial disorder or invasion of the rights of others is, of course, not immunized by the constitutional guarantee of freedom of speech.

Under our Constitution, free speech is not a right that is given only to be so circumscribed that it exists in principle, but not in fact. Freedom of expression would not truly exist if the right could be exercised only in an area that a benevolent government has provided as a safe haven for crackpots.

The Constitution says that Congress (and the States) may not abridge the right to free speech. This provision means what it says. We properly read it to permit reasonable regulation of speech-connected activities in carefully restricted circumstances. But we do not confine the permissible exercise of First Amendment rights to a telephone booth or the four corners of a pamphlet, or to supervised and ordained discussion in a school classroom. . . .

As we have discussed, the record does not demonstrate any facts which might reasonably have led school authorities to forecast substantial disruption of or material interference with school activities, and no disturbances or disorders on the school premises in fact occurred. These petitioners merely went about their ordained rounds in school. Their deviation consisted only in wearing on their sleeve a band of black cloth, not more than two inches wide. They wore it to exhibit their disapproval of the Vietnam hostilities and their advocacy of a truce, to make their views known, and, by their example, to influence others to adopt them. They neither interrupted school activities nor sought to intrude in the school affairs or the lives of others. They caused discussion outside of the classrooms, but no interference with work and no disorder. In the circumstances, our Constitution does not permit officials of the State to deny their form of expression.

We express no opinion as to the form of relief which should be granted, this being a matter for the lower courts to determine. We reverse and remand for further proceedings consistent with this opinion.

Reversed and remanded.

New York Times Company v. United States (1971)

> *The Supreme Court ruled in this case that the Nixon administration's efforts to block the publication of classified information violated the First Amendment guarantee of freedom of the press. The case is notable for its refusal to place national security over the guarantees of the First Amendment.*

PER CURIAM

We granted certiorari in these cases in which the United States seeks to enjoin the New York Times and the Washington Post from publishing the contents of a classified study entitled "History of U.S. Decision-Making Process on Viet Nam Policy."

"Any system of prior restraints of expression comes to this Court bearing a heavy presumption against its constitutional validity." The Government "thus carries a heavy burden of showing justification for the imposition of such a restraint." The District Court for the Southern District of New York, in the *New York Times* case, and the District Court for the District of Columbia and the Court of Appeals for the District of Columbia Circuit, in the *Washington Post* case, held that the Government had not met that burden. We agree.

The judgment of the Court of Appeals for the District of Columbia Circuit is therefore affirmed. The order of the Court of Appeals for the Second Circuit is reversed, and the case is remanded with directions to enter a judgment affirming the judgment of the District Court for the Southern District of New York. The stays entered June 25, 1971, by the Court are vacated. The judgments shall issue forthwith.

So ordered. . . .

MR. JUSTICE BLACK, with whom MR. JUSTICE DOUG-LAS joins, concurring.

I adhere to the view that the Government's case against the Washington Post should have been dismissed, and that the injunction against the New York Times should have been vacated without oral argument when the cases were first presented to this Court. I believe that every moment's continuance of the injunctions against these newspapers amounts to a flagrant, indefensible, and continuing violation of the First Amendment. . . .

Our Government was launched in 1789 with the adoption of the Constitution. The Bill of Rights, including the First Amendment, followed in 1791. Now, for the first time in the 182 years since the founding of the Republic, the federal courts are asked to hold that the First Amendment does not mean what it says, but rather means that the Government can halt the publication of current news of vital importance to the people of this country.

In seeking injunctions against these newspapers, and in its presentation to the Court, the Executive Branch seems to have forgotten the essential purpose and history of the First

Amendment. When the Constitution was adopted, many people strongly opposed it because the document contained no Bill of Rights to safeguard certain basic freedoms. They especially feared that the new powers granted to a central government might be interpreted to permit the government to curtail freedom of religion, press, assembly, and speech. In response to an overwhelming public clamor, James Madison offered a series of amendments to satisfy citizens that these great liberties would remain safe and beyond the power of government to abridge. . . .

In the First Amendment, the Founding Fathers gave the free press the protection it must have to fulfill its essential role in our democracy. The press was to serve the governed, not the governors. The Government's power to censor the press was abolished so that the press would remain forever free to censure the Government. The press was protected so that it could bare the secrets of government and inform the people. Only a free and unrestrained press can effectively expose deception in government. And paramount among the responsibilities of a free press is the duty to prevent any part of the government from deceiving the people and sending them off to distant lands to die of foreign fevers and foreign shot and shell. In my view, far from deserving condemnation for their courageous reporting, the New York Times, the Washington Post, and other newspapers should be commended for serving the purpose that the Founding Fathers saw so clearly. In revealing the workings of government that led to the Vietnam war, the newspapers nobly did precisely that which the Founders hoped and trusted they would do.

The Government's case here is based on premises entirely different from those that guided the Framers of the First Amendment. . . .

And the Government argues in its brief that, in spite of the First Amendment,

> "[t]he authority of the Executive Department to protect the nation against publication of information whose disclosure would endanger the national security stems from two interrelated sources: the constitutional power of the President over the conduct of foreign affairs and his authority as Commander-in-Chief." . . .

The word "security" is a broad, vague generality whose contours should not be invoked to abrogate the fundamental law embodied in the First Amendment. The guarding of military and diplomatic secrets at the expense of informed representative government provides no real security for our Republic. The Framers of the First Amendment, fully aware of both the need to defend a new nation and the abuses of the English and Colonial governments, sought to give this new society strength and security by providing that freedom of speech, press, religion, and assembly should not be abridged. . . .

Part IV

REPRODUCTIVE RIGHTS

─────────── ☆ ───────────

This part delves into one of the most contentious issues facing the Supreme Court and the nation today: the extent to which the Constitution protects a right to privacy in matters of reproductive freedom. Starting in 1965, the Court found that a right to privacy was implicit in the Bill of Rights and extended it to apply to the use of contraception free from government limits. In subsequent cases, the Court extended that right to privacy to a right to abortion. But now, a majority of the justices on the Court have indicated that these cases are mistaken, rolling back the right to privacy in the area of abortion. As you read these cases, think for yourself about their soundness and whether the Court would be limiting a constitutional freedom by limiting the right to privacy, as some hold.

Griswold v. Connecticut
(1965)

> *The Supreme Court ruled here that married couples could purchase contraceptives without government intervention or restriction. That right of "privacy" was later extended to unmarried couples and to reproductive freedoms more broadly, including the right to abortion.*

MR. JUSTICE DOUGLAS delivered the opinion of the Court.

Appellant Griswold is Executive Director of the Planned Parenthood League of Connecticut. Appellant Buxton is a licensed physician and a professor at the Yale Medical School who served as Medical Director for the League at its Center in New Haven—a center open and operating from November 1 to November 10, 1961, when appellants were arrested.

They gave information, instruction, and medical advice to *married persons* as to the means of preventing conception. They examined the wife and prescribed the best contraceptive device or material for her use. . . .

The statutes whose constitutionality is involved in this appeal are §§ 53-32 and 54-196 of the General Statutes of Connecticut. The former provides:

"Any person who uses any drug, medicinal article or instrument for the purpose of preventing conception shall be fined not less than fifty dollars or imprisoned not less than sixty days nor more than one year or be both fined and imprisoned."

Section 54-196 provides:

"Any person who assists, abets, counsels, causes, hires or commands another to commit any offense may be prosecuted and punished as if he were the principal offender."

The appellants were found guilty as accessories and fined $100 each, against the claim that the accessory statute, as so applied, violated the Fourteenth Amendment. . . .

We think that appellants have standing to raise the constitutional rights of the married people with whom they had a professional relationship. . . .

. . . This law . . . operates directly on an intimate relation of husband and wife and their physician's role in one aspect of that relation.

The association of people is not mentioned in the Constitution nor in the Bill of Rights. The right to educate a child in a school of the parents' choice—whether public or private or parochial—is also not mentioned. Nor is the right to study any particular subject or any foreign language. Yet the First Amendment has been construed to include certain of those rights. . . .

. . . In other words, the State may not, consistently with the spirit of the First Amendment, contract the spectrum of available knowledge. The right of freedom of speech and press includes not only the right to utter or to print, but the

right to distribute, the right to receive, the right to read and
freedom of inquiry, freedom of thought, and freedom to teach—
indeed, the freedom of the entire university community. . . .
Without those peripheral rights, the specific rights would be
less secure. . . .

. . . [T]he First Amendment has a penumbra where privacy is protected from governmental intrusion. . . .

The foregoing cases suggest that specific guarantees in the
Bill of Rights have penumbras, formed by emanations from
those guarantees that help give them life and substance. Various guarantees create zones of privacy. The right of association contained in the penumbra of the First Amendment is
one, as we have seen. The Third Amendment, in its prohibition against the quartering of soldiers "in any house" in time
of peace without the consent of the owner, is another facet of
that privacy. The Fourth Amendment explicitly affirms the
"right of the people to be secure in their persons, houses, pa-
pers, and effects, against unreasonable searches and sei-
zures." The Fifth Amendment, in its Self-Incrimination
Clause, enables the citizen to create a zone of privacy which
government may not force him to surrender to his detriment.
The Ninth Amendment provides: "The enumeration in the
Constitution, of certain rights, shall not be construed to deny
or disparage others retained by the people." . . .

We have had many controversies over these penumbral
rights of "privacy and repose." . . . These cases bear witness
that the right of privacy which presses for recognition here is
a legitimate one.

The present case, then, concerns a relationship lying
within the zone of privacy created by several fundamental
constitutional guarantees. And it concerns a law which, in
forbidding the use of contraceptives, rather than regulating
their manufacture or sale, seeks to achieve its goals by means

having a maximum destructive impact upon that relationship. Such a law cannot stand. . . . Would we allow the police to search the sacred precincts of marital bedrooms for telltale signs of the use of contraceptives? The very idea is repulsive to the notions of privacy surrounding the marriage relationship.

We deal with a right of privacy older than the Bill of Rights—older than our political parties, older than our school system. Marriage is a coming together for better or for worse, hopefully enduring, and intimate to the degree of being sacred. It is an association that promotes a way of life, not causes; a harmony in living, not political faiths; a bilateral loyalty, not commercial or social projects. Yet it is an association for as noble a purpose as any involved in our prior decisions.

Reversed.

Roe v. Wade
(1973)

In this case, the Supreme Court notably ruled that the Constitution protected the right of a pregnant woman to seek an abortion until the third trimester without excessive government interference or restriction until the third trimester. The decision remains among the most controversial of the Court's classic cases. Now overturned as a result of the decision in Dobbs v. Jackson Women's Health Organization *in 2022, it deserves close study. Readers should ask not just about the result in the case but about the Court's approach to thinking about liberty more generally in the Constitution. Do they agree with Justice Alito's claim in* Dobbs *that the* Roe *decision was "wrong the day it was decided"?*

MR. JUSTICE BLACKMUN delivered the opinion of the Court.

This Texas federal appeal and its Georgia companion present constitutional challenges to state criminal abortion legislation. The Texas statutes under attack here are typical of those that have been in effect in many States for approximately a century. The Georgia statutes, in contrast, have a modern cast, and are a legislative product that, to an extent at least, obviously reflects the influences of recent attitudinal change, of advancing medical knowledge and techniques, and of new thinking about an old issue.

We forthwith acknowledge our awareness of the sensitive and emotional nature of the abortion controversy, of the vigorous opposing views, even among physicians, and of the deep and seemingly absolute convictions that the subject inspires. One's philosophy, one's experiences, one's exposure to the raw edges of human existence, one's religious training, one's attitudes toward life and family and their values, and the moral standards one establishes and seeks to observe, are all likely to influence and to color one's thinking and conclusions about abortion. . . .

Our task, of course, is to resolve the issue by constitutional measurement, free of emotion and of predilection. We seek earnestly to do this, and, because we do, we have inquired into, and in this opinion place some emphasis upon, medical and medical-legal history and what that history reveals about man's attitudes toward the abortion procedure over the centuries. . . .

I

The Texas statutes that concern us here are Arts. 1191–1194 and 1196 of the State's Penal Code. These make it a crime to "procure an abortion," as therein defined, or to attempt one, except with respect to "an abortion procured or attempted by medical advice for the purpose of saving the life of the mother." Similar statutes are in existence in a majority of the States. . . .

II

Jane Roe, a single woman who was residing in Dallas County, Texas, instituted this federal action in March 1970 against the District Attorney of the county. She sought a declaratory judgment that the Texas criminal abortion statutes were unconstitutional on their face, and an injunction restraining the defendant from enforcing the statutes.

Roe alleged that she was unmarried and pregnant; that she wished to terminate her pregnancy by an abortion "performed by a competent, licensed physician, under safe, clinical conditions"; that she was unable to get a "legal" abortion in Texas because her life did not appear to be threatened by the continuation of her pregnancy; and that she could not afford to travel to another jurisdiction in order to secure a legal abortion under safe conditions. She claimed that the Texas statutes were unconstitutionally vague and that they abridged her right of personal privacy, protected by the First, Fourth, Fifth, Ninth, and Fourteenth Amendments. By an amendment to her complaint, Roe purported to sue "on behalf of herself and all other women" similarly situated. . . .

V

The principal thrust of appellant's attack on the Texas statutes is that they improperly invade a right, said to be possessed by the pregnant woman, to choose to terminate her pregnancy. Appellant would discover this right in the concept of personal "liberty" embodied in the Fourteenth Amendment's

Due Process Clause; or in personal, marital, familial, and sexual privacy said to be protected by the Bill of Rights or its penumbras. Before addressing this claim, we feel it desirable briefly to survey, in several aspects, the history of abortion, for such insight as that history may afford us, and then to examine the state purposes and interests behind the criminal abortion laws.

VI

It perhaps is not generally appreciated that the restrictive criminal abortion laws in effect in a majority of States today are of relatively recent vintage. Those laws, generally proscribing abortion or its attempt at any time during pregnancy except when necessary to preserve the pregnant woman's life, are not of ancient or even of common law origin. Instead, they derive from statutory changes effected, for the most part, in the latter half of the 19th century. . . .

It is thus apparent that, at common law, at the time of the adoption of our Constitution, and throughout the major portion of the 19th century, abortion was viewed with less disfavor than under most American statutes currently in effect. Phrasing it another way, a woman enjoyed a substantially broader right to terminate a pregnancy than she does in most States today. At least with respect to the early stage of pregnancy, and very possibly without such a limitation, the opportunity to make this choice was present in this country well into the 19th century. Even later, the law continued for some time to treat less punitively an abortion procured in early pregnancy. . . .

VIII

The Constitution does not explicitly mention any right of privacy. In a line of decisions, however, . . . the Court has recognized that a right of personal privacy, or a guarantee of certain areas or zones of privacy, does exist under the Constitution. . . . These decisions make it clear that only personal rights that can be deemed "fundamental" or "implicit in the concept of ordered liberty," are included in this guarantee of personal privacy. They also make it clear that the right has some extension to activities relating to marriage, procreation, contraception, family relationships, and childrearing and education.

This right of privacy, whether it be founded in the Fourteenth Amendment's concept of personal liberty and restrictions upon state action, as we feel it is, or, as the District Court determined, in the Ninth Amendment's reservation of rights to the people, is broad enough to encompass a woman's decision whether or not to terminate her pregnancy. The detriment that the State would impose upon the pregnant woman by denying this choice altogether is apparent. Specific and direct harm medically diagnosable even in early pregnancy may be involved. Maternity, or additional offspring, may force upon the woman a distressful life and future. Psychological harm may be imminent. Mental and physical health may be taxed by child care. There is also the distress, for all concerned, associated with the unwanted child, and there is the problem of bringing a child into a family already unable, psychologically and otherwise, to care for it. In other cases, as in this one, the additional difficulties and continuing stigma of unwed motherhood may be involved.

All these are factors the woman and her responsible physician necessarily will consider in consultation.

On the basis of elements such as these, appellant and some *amici* argue that the woman's right is absolute and that she is entitled to terminate her pregnancy at whatever time, in whatever way, and for whatever reason she alone chooses. With this we do not agree. . . . The Court's decisions recognizing a right of privacy also acknowledge that some state regulation in areas protected by that right is appropriate. As noted above, a State may properly assert important interests in safeguarding health, in maintaining medical standards, and in protecting potential life. At some point in pregnancy, these respective interests become sufficiently compelling to sustain regulation of the factors that govern the abortion decision. The privacy right involved, therefore, cannot be said to be absolute. . . .

We, therefore, conclude that the right of personal privacy includes the abortion decision, but that this right is not unqualified, and must be considered against important state interests in regulation. . . .

IX

. . . Appellee argues that the State's determination to recognize and protect prenatal life from and after conception constitutes a compelling state interest. As noted above, we do not agree fully with either formulation.

A. The appellee and certain *amici* argue that the fetus is a "person" within the language and meaning of the Fourteenth Amendment. In support of this, they outline at length and in detail the well-known facts of fetal development. If this suggestion of personhood is established, the appellant's case, of course, collapses, for the fetus' right to life would then be guaranteed specifically by the Amendment. . . .

The Constitution does not define "person" in so many words. Part 1 of the Fourteenth Amendment contains three references to "person." The first, in defining "citizens," speaks of "persons born or naturalized in the United States." The word also appears both in the Due Process Clause and in the Equal Protection Clause. "Person" is used in other places in the Constitution. . . . But in nearly all these instances, the use of the word is such that it has application only post-natally. None indicates, with any assurance, that it has any possible pre-natal application.

All this, together with our observation that, throughout the major portion of the 19th century, prevailing legal abortion practices were far freer than they are today, persuades us that the word "person," as used in the Fourteenth Amendment, does not include the unborn. . . .

Texas urges that, apart from the Fourteenth Amendment, life begins at conception and is present throughout pregnancy, and that, therefore, the State has a compelling interest in protecting that life from and after conception. We need not resolve the difficult question of when life begins. When those trained in the respective disciplines of medicine, philosophy, and theology are unable to arrive at any consensus, the judiciary, at this point in the development of man's knowledge, is not in a position to speculate as to the answer. . . .

X

In view of all this, we do not agree that, by adopting one theory of life, Texas may override the rights of the pregnant woman that are at stake. We repeat, however, that the State does have an important and legitimate interest in preserving and protecting the health of the pregnant woman, whether she be a resident of the State or a nonresident who seeks medical consultation and treatment there, and that it has still *another* important and legitimate interest in protecting the potentiality of human life. These interests are separate and distinct. Each grows in substantiality as the woman approaches term and, at a point during pregnancy, each becomes "compelling."

With respect to the State's important and legitimate interest in the health of the mother, the "compelling" point, in the light of present medical knowledge, is at approximately the end of the first trimester. This is so because of the now-established medical fact, that, until the end of the first trimester mortality in abortion may be less than mortality in normal childbirth. It follows that, from and after this point, a State may regulate the abortion procedure to the extent that the regulation reasonably relates to the preservation and protection of maternal health. Examples of permissible state regulation in this area are requirements as to the qualifications of the person who is to perform the abortion; as to the licensure of that person; as to the facility in which the procedure is to be performed, that is, whether it must be a hospital or may be a clinic or some other place of less-than-hospital status; as to the licensing of the facility; and the like.

This means, on the other hand, that, for the period of pregnancy prior to this "compelling" point, the attending physician, in consultation with his patient, is free to determine, without regulation by the State, that, in his medical judgment, the patient's pregnancy should be terminated. If that decision is reached, the judgment may be effectuated by an abortion free of interference by the State. . . .

Planned Parenthood v. Casey
(1992)

> *This case changed the standard courts used for reviewing*
> *abortion restrictions passed by states. Whereas* Roe v.
> Wade *required courts to review abortion restrictions*
> *under a standard of strict scrutiny, this case changed the*
> *standard to one that assessed whether such restrictions*
> *placed an "undue burden" on affected individuals. Al-*
> *though the case was a compromise to allow more abortion*
> *restrictions, it was overturned along with* Roe *in the*
> Dobbs *decision.*

I

Liberty finds no refuge in a jurisprudence of doubt. Yet 19 years after our holding that the Constitution protects a woman's right to terminate her pregnancy in its early stages, *Roe v. Wade* (1973), that definition of liberty is still questioned....

At issue in these cases are five provisions of the Pennsylvania Abortion Control Act of 1982, as amended in 1988 and 1989.... The Act requires that a woman seeking an abortion give her informed consent prior to the abortion procedure, and specifies that she be provided with certain information at least 24 hours before the abortion is performed. For a minor to obtain an abortion, the Act requires the informed consent of one of her parents, but provides for a judicial bypass option if the minor does not wish to or cannot obtain a parent's consent. Another provision of the Act requires that, unless certain exceptions apply, a married woman seeking an abortion must sign a statement indicating that she has notified her husband of her intended abortion. The Act exempts compliance with these three requirements in the event of a "medical emergency," which is defined in § 3203 of the Act. In addition to the above provisions regulating the performance of abortions, the Act imposes certain reporting requirements on facilities that provide abortion services.

Before any of these provisions took effect, the petitioners, who are five abortion clinics and one physician representing himself as well as a class of physicians who provide abortion services, brought this suit seeking declaratory and injunctive relief. Each provision was challenged as unconstitutional on its face. . . .

After considering the fundamental constitutional questions resolved by *Roe*, principles of institutional integrity, and the rule of *stare decisis*, we are led to conclude this: the essential holding of *Roe v. Wade* should be retained and once again reaffirmed.

It must be stated at the outset and with clarity that *Roe*'s essential holding, the holding we reaffirm, has three parts. First is a recognition of the right of the woman to choose to have an abortion before viability and to obtain it without undue interference from the State. Before viability, the State's interests are not strong enough to support a prohibition of abortion or the imposition of a substantial obstacle to the woman's effective right to elect the procedure. Second is a confirmation of the State's power to restrict abortions after fetal viability, if the law contains exceptions for pregnancies which endanger the woman's life or health. And third is the principle that the State has legitimate interests from the outset of the pregnancy in protecting the health of the woman and the life of the fetus that may become a child. These principles do not contradict one another; and we adhere to each.

II

Constitutional protection of the woman's decision to terminate her pregnancy derives from the Due Process Clause of the Fourteenth Amendment. It declares that no State shall "deprive any person of life, liberty, or property, without due process of law." The controlling word in the cases before us is "liberty." . . . As Justice Brandeis observed, ". . . it is settled that the due process clause of the Fourteenth Amendment applies to matters of substantive law as well as to matters of procedure. Thus all fundamental rights comprised within the term liberty are protected by the Federal Constitution from invasion by the States ." . . .

The most familiar of the substantive liberties protected by the Fourteenth Amendment are those recognized by the Bill of Rights. We have held that the Due Process Clause of the Fourteenth Amendment incorporates most of the Bill of Rights against the States. . . .

Men and women of good conscience can disagree, and we suppose some always shall disagree, about the profound moral and spiritual implications of terminating a pregnancy, even in its earliest stage. Some of us as individuals find abortion offensive to our most basic principles of morality, but that cannot control our decision. Our obligation is to define the liberty of all, not to mandate our own moral code. The underlying constitutional issue is whether the State can resolve these philosophic questions in such a definitive way that a woman lacks all choice in the matter, except perhaps in those rare circumstances in which the pregnancy is itself a danger to her own life or health, or is the result of rape or incest.

It is conventional constitutional doctrine that where reasonable people disagree the government can adopt one position or the other. That theorem, however, assumes a state of affairs in which the choice does not intrude upon a protected liberty. . . .

Our law affords constitutional protection to personal decisions relating to marriage, procreation, contraception, family relationships, child rearing, and education. . . . These matters, involving the most intimate and personal choices a person may make in a lifetime, choices central to personal dignity and autonomy, are central to the liberty protected by the Fourteenth Amendment. At the heart of liberty is the right to define one's own concept of existence, of meaning, of the universe, and of the mystery of human life. Beliefs about these matters could not define the attributes of personhood were they formed under compulsion of the State. . . .

. . . Abortion is a unique act. It is an act fraught with consequences for others: for the woman who must live with the implications of her decision; for the persons who perform and assist in the procedure; for the spouse, family, and society which must confront the knowledge that these procedures exist, procedures some deem nothing short of an act of violence against innocent human life; and, depending on one's beliefs, for the life or potential life that is aborted. Though abortion is conduct, it does not follow that the State is entitled to proscribe it in all instances. That is because the liberty of the woman is at stake in a sense unique to the human condition and so unique to the law. The mother who carries a child to full term is subject to anxieties, to physical constraints, to pain that only she must bear. That these sacrifices have from the beginning of the human race been endured by woman with a pride that ennobles her in the eyes of others and gives to the infant a bond of love cannot alone be grounds for the State to insist she make the sacrifice. . . .

It should be recognized, moreover, that in some critical respects the abortion decision is of the same character as the decision to use contraception, to which *Griswold v. Connecticut*, *Eisenstadt v. Baird*, and *Carey v. Population Services International* afford constitutional protection. We have no doubt as to the correctness of those decisions. They support the reasoning in *Roe* relating to the woman's liberty because they involve personal decisions concerning not only the meaning of procreation but also human responsibility and respect for it. . . .

It was this dimension of personal liberty that *Roe* sought to protect, and its holding invoked the reasoning and the tradition of the precedents we have discussed, granting protection to substantive liberties of the person. . . .

The Court's duty in the present cases is clear. In 1973, it confronted the already-divisive issue of governmental power to limit personal choice to undergo abortion, for which it provided a new resolution based on the due process guaranteed by the Fourteenth Amendment. Whether or not a new social consensus is developing on that issue, its divisiveness is no less today than in 1973, and pressure to overrule the decision, like pressure to retain it, has grown only more intense. A decision to overrule *Roe*'s essential holding under the existing circumstances would address error, if error there was, at the cost of both profound and unnecessary damage to the Court's legitimacy, and to the Nation's commitment to the rule of law. It is therefore imperative to adhere to the essence of *Roe*'s original decision, and we do so today.

IV

From what we have said so far it follows that it is a constitutional liberty of the woman to have some freedom to terminate her pregnancy. We conclude that the basic decision in *Roe* was based on a constitutional analysis which we cannot now repudiate. The woman's liberty is not so unlimited, however, that from the outset the State cannot show its concern for the life of the unborn, and at a later point in fetal development the State's interest in life has sufficient force so that the right of the woman to terminate the pregnancy can be restricted. . . .

We conclude the line should be drawn at viability, so that before that time the woman has a right to choose to terminate her pregnancy. We adhere to this principle for two reasons. First, as we have said, is the doctrine of *stare decisis*. Any judicial act of line-drawing may seem somewhat arbitrary, but *Roe* was a reasoned statement, elaborated with great care. We have twice reaffirmed it in the face of great opposition. . . .

The second reason is that the concept of viability, as we noted in *Roe*, is the time at which there is a realistic possibility of maintaining and nourishing a life outside the womb, so that the independent existence of the second life can in reason and all fairness be the object of state protection that now overrides the rights of the woman. Consistent with other constitutional norms, legislatures may draw lines which appear arbitrary without the necessity of offering a justification. But courts may not. We must justify the lines we draw. And there is no line other than viability which is more workable. . . .

Roe established a trimester framework to govern abortion

regulations. Under this elaborate but rigid construct, almost no regulation at all is permitted during the first trimester of pregnancy; regulations designed to protect the woman's health, but not to further the State's interest in potential life, are permitted during the second trimester; and during the third trimester, when the fetus is viable, prohibitions are permitted provided the life or health of the mother is not at stake. . . .

The trimester framework no doubt was erected to ensure that the woman's right to choose not become so subordinate to the State's interest in promoting fetal life that her choice exists in theory but not in fact. We do not agree, however, that the trimester approach is necessary to accomplish this objective. A framework of this rigidity was unnecessary and in its later interpretation sometimes contradicted the State's permissible exercise of its powers.

Though the woman has a right to choose to terminate or continue her pregnancy before viability, it does not at all follow that the State is prohibited from taking steps to ensure that this choice is thoughtful and informed. Even in the earliest stages of pregnancy, the State may enact rules and regulations designed to encourage her to know that there are philosophic and social arguments of great weight that can be brought to bear in favor of continuing the pregnancy to full term and that there are procedures and institutions to allow adoption of unwanted children as well as a certain degree of state assistance if the mother chooses to raise the child herself. . . . It follows that States are free to enact laws to provide a reasonable framework for a woman to make a decision that has such profound and lasting meaning. This, too, we find consistent with *Roe*'s central premises, and indeed the inevitable consequence of our holding that the State has an interest in protecting the life of the unborn. . . .

The very notion that the State has a substantial interest in potential life leads to the conclusion that not all regulations must be deemed unwarranted. Not all burdens on the right to decide whether to terminate a pregnancy will be undue. In our view, the undue burden standard is the appropriate means of reconciling the State's interest with the woman's constitutionally protected liberty. . . .

A finding of an undue burden is a shorthand for the conclusion that a state regulation has the purpose or effect of placing a substantial obstacle in the path of a woman seeking an abortion of a nonviable fetus. . . .

Unless it has that effect on her right of choice, a state measure designed to persuade her to choose childbirth over abortion will be upheld if reasonably related to that goal. Regulations designed to foster the health of a woman seeking an abortion are valid if they do not constitute an undue burden. . . .

VI

Our Constitution is a covenant running from the first generation of Americans to us and then to future generations. It is a coherent succession. Each generation must learn anew that the Constitution's written terms embody ideas and aspirations that must survive more ages than one. We accept our responsibility not to retreat from interpreting the full meaning of the covenant in light of all of our precedents. We invoke it once again to define the freedom guaranteed by the Constitution's own promise, the promise of liberty. . . .

Dobbs v. Jackson Women's Health Organization (2022)

In Dobbs, Justice Alito abruptly ended the decades-long protection of abortion rights. His argument that Roe was "egregiously wrong" relied on two main points. The first was that there was no basis in the Constitution's text for abortion rights. The second was that rights protected under a broad umbrella of liberty had to be "traditional" in the sense that there was a long-standing history of guaranteeing them. This part of the decision includes Alito's history of the abortion debate in the United States. The opinion is anemic in its conception of constitutional civil liberties, stripping out those that cannot be established through explicit protections. As you read, consider whether it is an approach compatible with other rights protected by the Constitution, especially in Griswold, which opened this section. It is also important to keep Alito's opinion in mind in the next section, where we examine the Court's protection of LGBTQ+ rights. Alito claims the right to abortion is qualitatively different from those rights, but the case is potentially the opening of an assault on them as well.

JUSTICE ALITO delivered the opinion of the Court.

Abortion presents a profound moral issue on which Americans hold sharply conflicting views. Some believe fervently that a human person comes into being at conception and that abortion ends an innocent life. Others feel just as strongly that any regulation of abortion invades a woman's right to control her own body and prevents women from achieving full equality. Still others in a third group think that abortion should be allowed under some but not all circumstances, and those within this group hold a variety of views about the particular restrictions that should be imposed.

For the first 185 years after the adoption of the Constitution, each State was permitted to address this issue in accordance with the views of its citizens. Then, in 1973, this Court decided *Roe v. Wade*. Even though the Constitution makes no mention of abortion, the Court held that it confers a broad right to obtain one. It did not claim that American law or the common law had ever recognized such a right, and its survey of history ranged from the constitutionally irrelevant (*e.g.,* its discussion of abortion in antiquity) to the plainly incorrect (*e.g.,* its assertion that abortion was probably never a crime under the common law). . . .

At the time of *Roe*, 30 States still prohibited abortion at all stages. In the years prior to that decision, about a third of the States had liberalized their laws, but *Roe* abruptly ended that political process. It imposed the same highly restrictive regime on the entire Nation, and it effectively struck down the abortion laws of every single State. As Justice Byron White aptly put it in his dissent, the decision represented the "exercise of raw judicial power," and it sparked a national controversy that has embittered our political culture for a half century.

Eventually, in *Planned Parenthood of Southeastern Pa. v. Casey*, the Court revisited *Roe*, . . . the opinion concluded that *stare decisis*, which calls for prior decisions to be followed in most instances, required adherence to what it called *Roe*'s "central holding"—that a State may not constitutionally protect fetal life before "viability"—even if that holding was wrong. Anything less, the opinion claimed, would undermine respect for this Court and the rule of law.

Paradoxically, the judgment in *Casey* did a fair amount of overruling. Several important abortion decisions were overruled *in toto*, and *Roe* itself was overruled in part. *Casey* threw out *Roe*'s trimester scheme and substituted a new rule of uncertain origin under which States were forbidden to adopt any regulation that imposed an "undue burden" on a woman's right to have an abortion. . . .

The State of Mississippi asks us to uphold the constitutionality of a law that generally prohibits an abortion after the 15th week of pregnancy—several weeks before the point at which a fetus is now regarded as "viable" outside the womb. In defending this law, the State's primary argument is that we should reconsider and overrule *Roe* and *Casey* and once again allow each State to regulate abortion as its citizens wish. On the other side, respondents and the Solicitor General ask us to reaffirm *Roe* and *Casey*, and they contend that the Mississippi law cannot stand if we do so. Allowing Mississippi to prohibit abortions after 15 weeks of pregnancy, they argue, "would be no different than overruling *Casey* and *Roe* entirely." They contend that "no half-measures" are available and that we must either reaffirm or overrule *Roe* and *Casey*.

We hold that *Roe* and *Casey* must be overruled. The Constitution makes no reference to abortion, and no such right is implicitly protected by any constitutional provision, including the one on which the defenders of *Roe* and *Casey* now chiefly rely—the Due Process Clause of the Fourteenth Amendment. That provision has been held to guarantee some rights that are not mentioned in the Constitution, but any such right must be "deeply rooted in this Nation's history and tradition" and "implicit in the concept of ordered liberty." . . .

The right to abortion does not fall within this category. Until the latter part of the 20th century, such a right was entirely unknown in American law. Indeed, when the Fourteenth Amendment was adopted, three quarters of the States made abortion a crime at all stages of pregnancy. The abortion right is also critically different from any other right that this Court has held to fall within the Fourteenth Amendment's protection of "liberty." *Roe*'s defenders characterize the abortion right as similar to the rights recognized in past decisions involving matters such as intimate sexual relations, contraception, and marriage, but abortion is fundamentally different, as both *Roe* and *Casey* acknowledged, because it destroys what those decisions called "fetal life" and what the law now before us describes as an "unborn human being."

Stare decisis, the doctrine on which *Casey*'s controlling opinion was based, does not compel unending adherence to *Roe*'s abuse of judicial authority. *Roe* was egregiously wrong from the start. Its reasoning was exceptionally weak, and the decision has had damaging consequences. And far from bringing about a national settlement of the abortion issue, *Roe* and *Casey* have enflamed debate and deepened division.

It is time to heed the Constitution and return the issue of abortion to the people's elected representatives. "The permissibility of abortion, and the limitations, upon it, are to be resolved like most important questions in our democracy: by citizens trying to persuade one another and then voting." . . . That is what the Constitution and the rule of law demand.

I

The law at issue in this case, Mississippi's Gestational Age Act. . . . : "Except in a medical emergency or in the case of a severe fetal abnormality, a person shall not intentionally or knowingly perform . . . or induce an abortion of an unborn human being if the probable gestational age of the unborn human being has been determined to be greater than fifteen (15) weeks." . . .

II

We begin by considering the critical question whether the Constitution, properly understood, confers a right to obtain an abortion . . . , and we address that question in three steps. First, we explain the standard that our cases have used in determining whether the Fourteenth Amendment's reference to "liberty" protects a particular right. Second, we examine whether the right at issue in this case is rooted in our Nation's history and tradition and whether it is an essential component of what we have described as "ordered liberty." Finally, we consider whether a right to obtain an abortion is part of a broader entrenched right that is supported by other precedents.

A

1

. . . The Constitution makes no express reference to a right to obtain an abortion, and therefore those who claim that it protects such a right must show that the right is somehow implicit in the constitutional text.

Roe, however, was remarkably loose in its treatment of the constitutional text. It held that the abortion right, which is not mentioned in the Constitution, is part of a right to privacy, which is also not mentioned. And that privacy right, *Roe* observed, had been found to spring from no fewer than five different constitutional provisions—the First, Fourth, Fifth, Ninth, and Fourteenth Amendments. . . .

. . . [T]hat the Fourteenth Amendment's Due Process Clause provides substantive, as well as procedural, protection for "liberty"—has long been controversial. But our decisions have held that the Due Process Clause protects two categories of substantive rights.

The first consists of rights guaranteed by the first eight Amendments. . . . The second category—which is the one in question here—comprises a select list of fundamental rights that are not mentioned anywhere in the Constitution.

In deciding whether a right falls into either of these categories, the Court has long asked whether the right is "deeply rooted in [our] history and tradition" and whether it is essential to our Nation's "scheme of ordered liberty." And in conducting this inquiry, we have engaged in a careful analysis of the history of the right at issue. . . .

In interpreting what is meant by the Fourteenth Amendment's reference to "liberty," we must guard against the natural human tendency to confuse what that Amendment protects with our own ardent views about the liberty that Americans should enjoy. That is why the Court has long been "reluctant" to recognize rights that are not mentioned in the Constitution. . . . As the Court cautioned in *Glucksberg*, "[w]e must . . . exercise the utmost care whenever we are asked to break new ground in this field, lest the liberty protected by the Due Process Clause be subtly transformed into the policy preferences of the Members of this Court." [internal quotation marks and citation omitted].

On occasion, when the Court has ignored the "[a]ppropriate limits" imposed by "'respect for the teachings of history,'" it has fallen into the freewheeling judicial policymaking that characterized discredited decisions such as *Lochner v. New York*. The Court must not fall prey to such an unprincipled approach. Instead, guided by the history and tradition that map the essential components of our Nation's concept of ordered liberty, we must ask what the *Fourteenth Amendment* means by the term "liberty." When we engage in that inquiry in the present case, the clear answer is that the Fourteenth Amendment does not protect the right to an abortion.

B

1

Until the latter part of the 20th century, there was no support in American law for a constitutional right to obtain an abortion. No state constitutional provision had recognized such a right. Until a few years before *Roe* was handed down, no federal or state court had recognized such a right. Nor had any scholarly treatise of which we are aware. And although law review articles are not reticent about advocating new rights, the earliest article proposing a constitutional right to abortion that has come to our attention was published only a few years before *Roe*.

Not only was there no support for such a constitutional right until shortly before *Roe*, but abortion had long been a *crime* in every single State. . . . By the time of the adoption of the Fourteenth Amendment, three-quarters of the States had made abortion a crime at any stage of pregnancy, and the remaining States would soon follow. . . .

2

a

We begin with the common law, under which abortion was a crime at least after "quickening"—*i.e.*, the first felt movement of the fetus in the womb, which usually occurs between the 16th and 18th week of pregnancy.

The "eminent common-law authorities *all* describe abortion after quickening as criminal. . . .

Sir Edward Coke's 17th-century treatise likewise asserted that abortion of a quick child was "murder" if the "childe be born alive" and a "great misprision" if the "childe dieth in her body." Two treatises by Sir Matthew Hale likewise described abortion of a quick child who died in the womb as a "great crime" and a "great misprision." And writing near the time of the adoption of our Constitution, William Blackstone explained that abortion of a "quick" child was "by the ancient law homicide or manslaughter." . . .

In sum, although common-law authorities differed on the

severity of punishment for abortions committed at different points in pregnancy, none endorsed the practice. Moreover, we are aware of no common-law case or authority, and the parties have not pointed to any, that remotely suggests a positive *right* to procure an abortion at any stage of pregnancy.

b

In this country, the historical record is similar. . . . Manuals for justices of the peace printed in the Colonies in the 18th century typically restated the common-law rule on abortion, and some manuals repeated Hale's and Blackstone's statements that anyone who prescribed medication "unlawfully to destroy the child" would be guilty of murder if the woman died.

The few cases available from the early colonial period corroborate that abortion was a crime. . . . And by the 19th century, courts frequently explained that the common law made abortion of a quick child a crime. . . .

In this country during the 19th century, the vast majority of the States enacted statutes criminalizing abortion at all stages of pregnancy. . . .

The trend in the Territories that would become the last 13 States was similar: All of them criminalized abortion at all stages of pregnancy between 1850 (the Kingdom of Hawaii) and 1919 (New Mexico). By the end of the 1950s, according to the *Roe* Court's own count, statutes in all but four States and the District of Columbia prohibited abortion "however and whenever performed, unless done to save or preserve the life of the mother."

This overwhelming consensus endured until the day *Roe* was decided. At that time, also by the *Roe* Court's own count, a substantial majority—30 States—still prohibited abortion at all stages except to save the life of the mother. And though *Roe* discerned a "trend toward liberalization" in about "one-third of the States," those States still criminalized some abortions and regulated them more stringently than *Roe* would allow.

d

The inescapable conclusion is that a right to abortion is not deeply rooted in the Nation's history and traditions. On the contrary, an unbroken tradition of prohibiting abortion on pain of criminal punishment persisted from the earliest days of the common law until 1973. . . .

Instead of seriously pressing the argument that the abortion right itself has deep roots, supporters of *Roe* and *Casey* contend that the abortion right is an integral part of a broader entrenched right. *Roe* termed this a right to privacy, and *Casey* described it as the freedom to make "intimate and personal choices" that are "central to personal dignity and autonomy." *Casey* elaborated: "At the heart of liberty is the right to define one's own concept of existence, of meaning, of the universe, and of the mystery of human life." . . .

Ordered liberty sets limits and defines the boundary between competing interests. *Roe* and *Casey* each struck a particular balance between the interests of a woman who wants an abortion and the interests of what they termed "potential life." But the people of the various States may evaluate those interests differently. . . . Our Nation's historical understanding of ordered liberty does not prevent the people's elected representatives from deciding how abortion should be regulated. . . .

What sharply distinguishes the abortion right from the

rights recognized in the cases on which *Roe* and *Casey* rely is something that both those decisions acknowledged: Abortion destroys what those decisions call "potential life" and what the law at issue in this case regards as the life of an "unborn human being." None of the other decisions cited by *Roe* and *Casey* involved the critical moral question posed by abortion. They are therefore inapposite. They do not support the right to obtain an abortion, and by the same token, our conclusion that the Constitution does not confer such a right does not undermine them in any way. . . .

III

We next consider whether the doctrine of *stare decisis* counsels continued acceptance of *Roe* and *Casey*. *Stare decisis* plays an important role in our case law, and we have explained that it serves many valuable ends. It protects the interests of those who have taken action in reliance on a past decision. . . . It fosters "evenhanded" decisionmaking by requiring that like cases be decided in a like manner. It "contributes to the actual and perceived integrity of the judicial process." And it restrains judicial hubris and reminds us to respect the judgment of those who have grappled with important questions in the past. . . .

We have long recognized, however, that *stare decisis* is "not an inexorable command," and it "is at its weakest when we interpret the Constitution." It has been said that it is sometimes more important that an issue "'be settled than that it be settled right.'" But when it comes to the interpretation of the Constitution—the "great charter of our liberties," which was meant "to endure through a long lapse of ages"—we place a high value on having the matter "settled right." . . .

Some of our most important constitutional decisions have overruled prior precedents. We mention three. In *Brown v. Board of Education*, the Court repudiated the "separate but equal" doctrine, which had allowed States to maintain racially segregated schools and other facilities. In so doing, the Court overruled the infamous decision in *Plessy v. Ferguson*, along with six other Supreme Court precedents that had applied the separate-but-equal rule. . . .

Roe was on a collision course with the Constitution from the day it was decided, *Casey* perpetuated its errors, and those errors do not concern some arcane corner of the law of little importance to the American people. Rather, wielding nothing but "raw judicial power," the Court usurped the power to address a question of profound moral and social importance that the Constitution unequivocally leaves for the people. . . . The Court short-circuited the democratic process by closing it to the large number of Americans who dissented in any respect from *Roe*. . . . Together, *Roe* and *Casey* represent an error that cannot be allowed to stand. . . .

C

Workability. Our precedents counsel that another important consideration in deciding whether a precedent should be overruled is whether the rule it imposes is workable—that is, whether it can be understood and applied in a consistent and predictable manner. *Casey*'s "undue burden" test has scored poorly on the workability scale.

1

Problems begin with the very concept of an "undue burden." As Justice Scalia noted in his *Casey* partial dissent, determining whether a burden is "due" or "undue" is "inherently standardless." . . .

Having shown that traditional *stare decisis* factors do not weigh in favor of retaining *Roe* or *Casey*, we must address one final argument that featured prominently in the *Casey* plurality opinion.

The argument was cast in different terms, but stated simply, it was essentially as follows. The American people's belief in the rule of law would be shaken if they lost respect for this Court as an institution that decides important cases based on principle, not "social and political pressures." There is a special danger that the public will perceive a decision as having been made for unprincipled reasons when the Court overrules a controversial "watershed" decision, such as *Roe*. A decision overruling *Roe* would be perceived as having been made "under fire" and as a "surrender to political pressure," and therefore the preservation of public approval of the Court weighs heavily in favor of retaining *Roe*.

This analysis starts out on the right foot but ultimately veers off course. The *Casey* plurality was certainly right that it is important for the public to perceive that our decisions are based on principle, and we should make every effort to achieve that objective by issuing opinions that carefully show how a proper understanding of the law leads to the results we reach. But we cannot exceed the scope of our authority under the Constitution, and we cannot allow our decisions to be affected by any extraneous influences such as concern about the public's reaction to our work. . . . The doctrine of *stare decisis* is an adjunct of this duty, and should be no more subject to the vagaries of public opinion than is the basic judicial task." In suggesting otherwise, the *Casey* plurality went beyond this Court's role in our constitutional system. . . .

We do not pretend to know how our political system or society will respond to today's decision overruling *Roe* and *Casey*. And even if we could foresee what will happen, we would have no authority to let that knowledge influence our decision. We can only do our job, which is to interpret the law, apply longstanding principles of *stare decisis*, and decide this case accordingly.

We therefore hold that the Constitution does not confer a right to abortion. *Roe* and *Casey* must be overruled, and the authority to regulate abortion must be returned to the people and their elected representatives. . . .

JUSTICE BREYER, JUSTICE SOTOMAYOR, and JUSTICE KAGAN, dissenting.

For half a century, *Roe v. Wade*, and *Planned Parenthood of Southeastern Pa. v. Casey*, have protected the liberty and equality of women. *Roe* held, and *Casey* reaffirmed, that the Constitution safeguards a woman's right to decide for herself whether to bear a child. *Roe* held, and *Casey* reaffirmed, that in the first stages of pregnancy, the government could not make that choice for women. The government could not control a woman's body or the course of a woman's life: It could not determine what the woman's future would be. Respecting a woman as an autonomous being, and granting her full equality, meant giving her substantial choice over this most personal and most consequential of all life decisions.

Roe and *Casey* well understood the difficulty and divisiveness of the abortion issue. The Court knew that Americans hold profoundly different views about the "moral[ity]" of "terminating a pregnancy, even in its earliest stage." . . . So the Court struck a balance, as it often does when values and goals compete. It held that the State could prohibit abortions after fetal viability, so long as the ban contained exceptions to safeguard a woman's life or health. It held that even before viability, the State could regulate the abortion procedure in multiple and meaningful ways. But until the viability line was crossed, the Court held, a State could not impose a "substantial obstacle" on a woman's "right to elect the procedure" as she (not the government) thought proper, in light of all the circumstances and complexities of her own life.

Today, the Court discards that balance. It says that from the very moment of fertilization, a woman has no rights to speak of. A State can force her to bring a pregnancy to term, even at the steepest personal and familial costs. . . . States will feel free to enact all manner of restrictions. The Mississippi law at issue here bars abortions after the 15th week of pregnancy. Under the majority's ruling, though, another State's law could do so after ten weeks, or five or three or one—or, again, from the moment of fertilization. States have already passed such laws, in anticipation of today's ruling. More will follow. Some States have enacted laws extending to all forms of abortion procedure, including taking medication in one's own home. They have passed laws without any exceptions for when the woman is the victim of rape or incest. Under those laws, a woman will have to bear her rapist's child or a young girl her father's—no matter if doing so will destroy her life. So too, after today's ruling, some States may compel women to carry to term a fetus with severe physical anomalies. . . .

States may even argue that a prohibition on abortion need make no provision for protecting a woman from risk of death or physical harm. Across a vast array of circumstances, a State will be able to impose its moral choice on a woman and coerce her to give birth to a child.

Enforcement of all these draconian restrictions will also be left largely to the States' devices. . . . Perhaps, in the wake of today's decision, a state law will criminalize the woman's conduct too, incarcerating or fining her for daring to seek or obtain an abortion. And as Texas has recently shown, a State can turn neighbor against neighbor, enlisting fellow citizens in the effort to root out anyone who tries to get an abortion, or to assist another in doing so.

The majority tries to hide the geographically expansive effects of its holding. Today's decision, the majority says, permits "each State" to address abortion as it pleases. That is cold comfort, of course, for the poor woman who cannot get the money to fly to a distant State for a procedure. Above all others, women lacking financial resources will suffer from today's decision. In any event, interstate restrictions will also soon be in the offing. After this decision, some States may block women from traveling out of State to obtain abortions, or even from receiving abortion medications from out of State. Some may criminalize efforts, including the provision of information or funding, to help women gain access to other States' abortion services. Most threatening of all, no language in today's decision stops the Federal Government from prohibiting abortions nationwide, once again from the moment of conception and without exceptions for rape or incest. If that happens, "the views of [an individual State's] citizens" will not matter. The challenge for a woman will be to finance a trip not to "New York [or] California" but to Toronto.

Whatever the exact scope of the coming laws, one result of today's decision is certain: the curtailment of women's rights, and of their status as free and equal citizens. Yesterday, the Constitution guaranteed that a woman confronted with an unplanned pregnancy could (within reasonable limits) make her own decision about whether to bear a child, with all the life-transforming consequences that act involves. And in thus safeguarding each woman's reproductive freedom, the Constitution also protected "[t]he ability of women to participate equally in [this Nation's] economic and social life." But no longer. As of today, this Court holds, a State can always force a woman to give birth, prohibiting even the earliest abortions. A State can thus transform what, when freely undertaken, is a wonder into what, when forced, may be a nightmare. Some women, especially women of means, will find ways around the State's assertion of power. Others—those without money or childcare or the ability to take time off from work—will not be so fortunate. Maybe they will try an unsafe method of abortion, and come to physical harm, or even die. Maybe they will undergo pregnancy and have a child, but at significant personal or familial cost. At the least, they will incur the cost of losing control of their lives. The Constitution will, today's majority holds, provide no shield, despite its guarantees of liberty and equality for all.

And no one should be confident that this majority is done with its work. The right *Roe* and *Casey* recognized does not stand alone. To the contrary, the Court has linked it for decades to other settled freedoms involving bodily integrity, familial relationships, and procreation. Most obviously, the right to terminate a pregnancy arose straight out of the right to purchase and use contraception. In turn, those rights led, more recently, to rights of same-sex intimacy and marriage. . . . The lone rationale for what the majority does today is that the right to elect an abortion is not "deeply rooted in history": Not until *Roe*, the majority argues, did people think abortion fell within the Constitution's guarantee of liberty. The same could be said, though, of most of the rights the majority claims it is not tampering with. The majority could write just as long an opinion showing, for example, that until the mid-20th century, "there was no support in American law for a constitutional right to obtain [contraceptives].". . . [A]ll rights that have no history stretching back to the mid-19th century are insecure. Either the mass of the majority's opinion is hypocrisy, or additional constitutional rights are under threat. It is one or the other.

One piece of evidence on that score seems especially salient: The majority's cavalier approach to overturning this Court's precedents. *Stare decisis* is the Latin phrase for a foundation stone of the rule of law: that things decided should stay decided unless there is a very good reason for change. It is a doctrine of judicial modesty and humility. Those qualities are not evident in today's opinion. The majority has no good reason for the upheaval in law and society it sets off. *Roe* and *Casey* have been the law of the land for decades, shaping women's expectations of their choices when an unplanned pregnancy occurs. Women have relied on the availability of abortion both in structuring their relationships and in planning their lives. The legal framework *Roe* and *Casey* developed to balance the competing interests in this sphere has proved workable in courts across the country. No recent developments, in either law or fact, have eroded or cast doubt on those precedents. Nothing, in short, has changed. . . . The Court reverses course today for one reason and one reason only: because the composition of this Court has changed. *Stare decisis*, this Court has often said, "contributes to the actual and perceived integrity of the judicial process" by ensuring that decisions are "founded in the law rather than in the proclivities of individuals." Today, the proclivities of individuals rule. The Court departs from its obligation to faithfully and impartially apply the law. We dissent.

Part V

LGBTQ+ RIGHTS

———— ☆ ————

A relatively recent development in Supreme Court history is the protection of the rights of LGBTQ+ people. This part begins with the Supreme Court's opinion in *Bowers v. Hardwick*, which upheld a law criminalizing oral and anal sex. The Court's subsequent rulings regulated that case to the legal Dark Ages, akin to *Plessy* in that it was clearly reversed. But after *Dobbs*, the direction the Court will take in this area is uncertain. While LGBTQ+ rights were expanded under the umbrella of *Griswold*'s privacy protections, the logic of that case is arguably under assault in *Dobbs*. Could LGBTQ+ rights be the next area where the Court will reverse course from its precedents protecting liberty? The possibility looms on the horizon, making it more urgent that citizen readers study these cases, thinking about how these rights might be defended.

Bowers v. Hardwick
(1986)

This case upheld the constitutionality of a Georgia law that prohibited what it called "sodomy," or oral and anal sex between consenting individuals. The case was centered on the constitutionality of prohibiting homosexual activity, though the law itself did not differentiate between homosexual and heterosexual sex acts. The case stands as an example of a precedent that once set the law of the land in the area of LGBTQ+ rights before it was reversed and a new era of gay rights was ushered in by the Supreme Court.

JUSTICE WHITE delivered the opinion of the Court.

In August, 1982, respondent Hardwick (hereafter respondent) was charged with violating the Georgia statute criminalizing sodomy by committing that act with another adult male in the bedroom of respondent's home. . . .

. . . The issue presented is whether the Federal Constitution confers a fundamental right upon homosexuals to engage in sodomy, and hence invalidates the laws of the many States that still make such conduct illegal, and have done so for a very long time. The case also calls for some judgment about the limits of the Court's role in carrying out its constitutional mandate.

We first register our disagreement with the Court of Appeals and with respondent that the Court's prior cases have construed the Constitution to confer a right of privacy that extends to homosexual sodomy and, for all intents and purposes, have decided this case. The reach of this line of cases was sketched in *Carey v. Population Services International.* *Pierce v. Society of Sisters* and *Meyer v. Nebraska* were described as dealing with childrearing and education; *Prince v. Massachusetts* with family relationships; *Skinner v. Oklahoma ex rel. Williamson* with procreation; *Loving v. Virginia* with marriage; *Griswold v. Connecticut* and *Eisenstadt v. Baird* with contraception; and *Roe v. Wade* with abortion. The latter three cases were interpreted as construing the Due Process Clause of the Fourteenth Amendment to confer a fundamental individual right to decide whether or not to beget or bear a child.

Accepting the decisions in these cases and the above description of them, we think it evident that none of the rights announced in those cases bears any resemblance to the claimed constitutional right of homosexuals to engage in acts of sodomy that is asserted in this case. No connection between family, marriage, or procreation, on the one hand, and homosexual activity, on the other, has been demonstrated, either by the Court of Appeals or by respondent. Moreover, any claim that these cases nevertheless stand for the proposition that any kind of private sexual conduct between consenting adults is constitutionally insulated from state proscription is unsupportable. Indeed, the Court's opinion in *Carey* twice asserted that the privacy right, which the *Griswold* line of cases found to be one of the protections provided by the Due Process Clause, did not reach so far.

Precedent aside, however, respondent would have us announce, as the Court of Appeals did, a fundamental right to engage in homosexual sodomy. This we are quite unwilling to do. It is true that, despite the language of the Due Process Clauses of the Fifth and Fourteenth Amendments, which appears to focus only on the processes by which life, liberty, or property is taken, the cases are legion in which those Clauses have been interpreted to have substantive content, subsuming rights that to a great extent are immune from federal or state regulation or proscription. Among such cases are those recognizing rights that have little or no textual support in the constitutional language. *Meyer*, *Prince*, and *Pierce* fall in this category, as do the privacy cases from *Griswold* to *Carey*.

Striving to assure itself and the public that announcing rights not readily identifiable in the Constitution's text involves much more than the imposition of the Justices' own choice of values on the States and the Federal Government, the Court has sought to identify the nature of the rights qualifying for heightened judicial protection. In *Palko v. Connecticut*, it was said that this category includes those fundamental liberties that are "implicit in the concept of ordered liberty," such that "neither liberty nor justice would exist if [they] were sacrificed." A different description of fundamental liberties appeared in *Moore v. East Cleveland*, where they are characterized as those liberties that are "deeply rooted in this Nation's history and tradition."

It is obvious to us that neither of these formulations would extend a fundamental right to homosexuals to engage in acts of consensual sodomy. Proscriptions against that conduct have ancient roots. Sodomy was a criminal offense at common law, and was forbidden by the laws of the original 13 States when they ratified the Bill of Rights. In 1868, when the Fourteenth Amendment was ratified, all but 5 of the 37 States in the Union had criminal sodomy laws. In fact, until 1961, all 50 States outlawed sodomy, and today, 24 States and the District of Columbia continue to provide criminal penalties for sodomy performed in private and between consenting adults. Against this background, to claim that a right to engage in such conduct is "deeply rooted in this Nation's history and tradition" or "implicit in the concept of ordered liberty" is, at best, facetious.

Nor are we inclined to take a more expansive view of our authority to discover new fundamental rights imbedded in the Due Process Clause. The Court is most vulnerable and comes nearest to illegitimacy when it deals with judge-made constitutional law having little or no cognizable roots in the language or design of the Constitution. That this is so was painfully demonstrated by the face-off between the Executive and the Court in the 1930's, which resulted in the repudiation of much of the substantive gloss that the Court had placed on the Due Process Clauses of the Fifth and Fourteenth Amendments. There should be, therefore, great resistance to expand the substantive reach of those Clauses, particularly if it requires redefining the category of rights deemed to be fundamental. Otherwise, the Judiciary necessarily takes to itself further authority to govern the country without express constitutional authority. The claimed right pressed on us today falls far short of overcoming this resistance. . . .

CHIEF JUSTICE BURGER, concurring.

I join the Court's opinion, but I write separately to underscore my view that, in constitutional terms, there is no such thing as a fundamental right to commit homosexual sodomy.

As the Court notes, the proscriptions against sodomy have very "ancient roots." Decisions of individuals relating to homosexual conduct have been subject to state intervention throughout the history of Western civilization. Condemnation of those practices is firmly rooted in Judeo-Christian moral and ethical standards. Homosexual sodomy was a capital crime under Roman law. During the English Reformation, when powers of the ecclesiastical courts were transferred to the King's Courts, the first English statute criminalizing sodomy was passed. Blackstone described "the infamous *crime against nature*" as an offense of "deeper malignity" than rape, a heinous act "the very mention of which is a disgrace to human nature," and "a crime not fit to be named." The common law of England, including its prohibition of sodomy, became the received law of Georgia and the other Colonies. In 1816, the Georgia Legislature passed the statute at issue here, and that statute has been continuously in force in one form or another since that time. To hold that the act of homosexual sodomy is somehow protected as a fundamental right would be to cast aside millennia of moral teaching.

This is essentially not a question of personal "preferences," but rather of the legislative authority of the State. I find nothing in the Constitution depriving a State of the power to enact the statute challenged here.

JUSTICE BLACKMUN, with whom JUSTICE BRENNAN, JUSTICE MARSHALL, and JUSTICE STEVENS join, dissenting.

This case is no more about "a fundamental right to engage in homosexual sodomy," as the Court purports to declare, than *Stanley v. Georgia* was about a fundamental right to watch obscene movies, or *Katz v. United States* was about a fundamental right to place interstate bets from a telephone booth. Rather, this case is about "the most comprehensive of rights and the right most valued by civilized men," namely, "the right to be let alone."

The statute at issue, Ga.Code Ann. § 16-6-2 (1984), denies individuals the right to decide for themselves whether to engage in particular forms of private, consensual sexual activity. The Court concludes that § 16-6-2 is valid essentially because "the laws of . . . many States . . . still make such conduct illegal and have done so for a very long time." But the fact that the moral judgments expressed by statutes like § 16-6-2 may be "'natural and familiar . . . ought not to conclude our judgment upon the question whether statutes embodying them conflict with the Constitution of the United States.'"

Like Justice Holmes, I believe that "[i]t is revolting to have no better reason for a rule of law than that so it was laid down in the time of Henry IV. It is still more revolting if the grounds upon which it was laid down have vanished long since, and the rule simply persists from blind imitation of the past."

I believe we must analyze respondent Hardwick's claim in the light of the values that underlie the constitutional right to privacy. If that right means anything, it means that, before Georgia can prosecute its citizens for making choices about the most intimate aspects of their lives, it must do more than assert that the choice they have made is an *"abominable crime not fit to be named among Christians."* . . .

First, the Court's almost obsessive focus on homosexual activity is particularly hard to justify in light of the broad language Georgia has used. Unlike the Court, the Georgia Legislature has not proceeded on the assumption that homosexuals are so different from other citizens that their lives may be controlled in a way that would not be tolerated if it limited the choices of those other citizens. Rather, Georgia has provided that "[a] person commits the offense of sodomy when he performs or submits to any sexual act involving the sex organs of one person and the mouth or anus of another."

The sex or status of the persons who engage in the act is irrelevant as a matter of state law. In fact, to the extent I can discern a legislative purpose for Georgia's 1968 enactment of § 16-6-2, that purpose seems to have been to broaden the coverage of the law to reach heterosexual as well as homosexual activity. I therefore see no basis for the Court's decision to treat this case as an "as applied" challenge to § 16-6-2, or for Georgia's attempt, both in its brief and at oral argument, to defend § 16-6-2 solely on the grounds that it prohibits homosexual activity. Michael Hardwick's standing may rest in significant part on Georgia's apparent willingness to enforce against homosexuals a law it seems not to have any desire to enforce against heterosexuals. But his claim that § 16-6-2 involves an unconstitutional intrusion into his privacy and his right of intimate association does not depend in any way on his sexual orientation. . . .

"Our cases long have recognized that the Constitution embodies a promise that a certain private sphere of individual liberty will be kept largely beyond the reach of government."

In construing the right to privacy, the Court has proceeded along two somewhat distinct, albeit complementary, lines. First, it has recognized a privacy interest with reference to certain decisions that are properly for the individual to make. Second, it has recognized a privacy interest with reference to certain places without regard for the particular activities in which the individuals who occupy them are engaged. The case before us implicates both the decisional and the spatial aspects of the right to privacy. . . .

The Court concludes today that none of our prior cases dealing with various decisions that individuals are entitled to make free of governmental interference "bears any resemblance to the claimed constitutional right of homosexuals to engage in acts of sodomy that is asserted in this case." While it is true that these cases may be characterized by their connection to protection of the family, the Court's conclusion that they extend no further than this boundary ignores the warning in *Moore v. East Cleveland* against "clos[ing] our eyes to the basic reasons why certain rights associated with the family have been accorded shelter under the Fourteenth Amendment's Due Process Clause."

We protect those rights not because they contribute, in some direct and material way, to the general public welfare, but because they form so central a part of an individual's life. "[T]he concept of privacy embodies the *'moral fact that a person belongs to himself, and not others nor to society as a whole.'" And so we protect the decision whether to marry precisely because marriage* "is an association that promotes a way of life, not causes; a harmony in living, not political faiths; a bilateral loyalty, not commercial or social projects." We protect the decision whether to have a child because parenthood alters so dramatically an individual's self-definition, not because of demographic considerations or the Bible's command to be fruitful and multiply. And we protect the family because it contributes so powerfully to the happiness of individuals, not because of a preference for stereotypical households. The Court recognized in *Roberts* that the "ability independently to define one's identity that is central to any concept of liberty" cannot truly be exercised in a vacuum; we all depend on the "emotional enrichment from close ties with others."

Only the most willful blindness could obscure the fact that sexual intimacy is "a sensitive, key relationship of human existence, central to family life, community welfare, and the development of human personality." The fact that individuals define themselves in a significant way through their intimate sexual relationships with others suggests, in a Nation as diverse as ours, that there may be many "right" ways of conducting those relationships, and that much of the richness of a relationship will come from the freedom an individual has to choose the form and nature of these intensely personal bonds.

In a variety of circumstances, we have recognized that a necessary corollary of giving individuals freedom to choose how to conduct their lives is acceptance of the fact that different individuals will make different choices. For example, in holding that the clearly important state interest in public education should give way to a competing claim by the Amish to the effect that extended formal schooling threatened their way of life, the Court declared:

> "There can be no assumption that today's majority is 'right' and the Amish and others like them are 'wrong.' A way of life that is odd or even erratic, but interferes with no rights or interests of others, is not to be condemned because it is different."

The Court claims that its decision today merely refuses to recognize a fundamental right to engage in homosexual sodomy; what the Court really has refused to recognize is the fundamental interest all individuals have in controlling the nature of their intimate associations with others.

Romer v. Evans
(1996)

> *In a 6–3 decision, the Supreme Court ruled that a state constitutional amendment from Colorado that prohibited extending protections to gay or bisexual people violated the Fourteenth Amendment's Equal Protection Clause.*

JUSTICE KENNEDY delivered the opinion of the Court.

One century ago, the first Justice Harlan admonished this Court that the Constitution "neither knows nor tolerates classes among citizens." Unheeded then, those words now are understood to state a commitment to the law's neutrality where the rights of persons are at stake. The Equal Protection Clause enforces this principle and today requires us to hold invalid a provision of Colorado's Constitution. . . .

The enactment challenged in this case is an amendment to the Constitution of the State of Colorado, adopted in a 1992 statewide referendum. The parties and the state courts refer to it as "Amendment 2," its designation when submitted to the voters. The impetus for the amendment and the contentious campaign that preceded its adoption came in large part from ordinances that had been passed in various Colorado municipalities. . . . What gave rise to the statewide controversy was the protection the ordinances afforded to persons discriminated against by reason of their sexual orientation. Amendment 2 repeals these ordinances to the extent they prohibit discrimination on the basis of "homosexual, lesbian or bisexual orientation, conduct, practices or relationships."

Yet Amendment 2, in explicit terms, does more than repeal or rescind these provisions. It prohibits all legislative, executive or judicial action at any level of state or local government designed to protect the named class, a class we shall refer to as homosexual persons or gays and lesbians. . . .

The State's principal argument in defense of Amendment 2 is that it puts gays and lesbians in the same position as all other persons. So, the State says, the measure does no more than deny homosexuals special rights. This reading of the amendment's language is implausible. . . .

Sweeping and comprehensive is the change in legal status effected by this law. So much is evident from the ordinances that the Colorado Supreme Court declared would be void by operation of Amendment 2. Homosexuals, by state decree, are put in a solitary class with respect to transactions and relations in both the private and governmental spheres. The amendment withdraws from homosexuals, but no others, specific legal protection from the injuries caused by discrimination, and it forbids reinstatement of these laws and policies.

The change that Amendment 2 works in the legal status of gays and lesbians in the private sphere is far reaching, both on its own terms and when considered in light of the structure and operation of modern antidiscrimination laws. . . .

Amendment 2 bars homosexuals from securing protection against the injuries that these public accommodations laws address. That in itself is a severe consequence, but there is more. Amendment 2, in addition, nullifies specific legal protections for this targeted class in all transactions in housing, sale of real estate, insurance, health and welfare services, private education, and employment.

Not confined to the private sphere, Amendment 2 also operates to repeal and forbid all laws or policies providing specific protection for gays or lesbians from discrimination by every level of Colorado government. . . .

The Fourteenth Amendment's promise that no person shall be denied the equal protection of the laws must coexist with the practical necessity that most legislation classifies for one purpose or another, with resulting disadvantage to various groups or persons. We have attempted to reconcile the principle with the reality by stating that, if a law neither burdens a fundamental right nor targets a suspect class, we will uphold the legislative classification so long as it bears a rational relation to some legitimate end.

Amendment 2 fails, indeed defies, even this conventional inquiry. First, the amendment has the peculiar property of imposing a broad and undifferentiated disability on a single named group, an exceptional and, as we shall explain, invalid form of legislation. Second, its sheer breadth is so discontinuous with the reasons offered for it that the amendment seems inexplicable by anything but animus toward the class that it affects; it lacks a rational relationship to legitimate state interests. . . .

. . . It is at once too narrow and too broad. It identifies persons by a single trait and then denies them protection across the board. The resulting disqualification of a class of persons from the right to seek specific protection from the law is unprecedented in our jurisprudence. . . .

It is not within our constitutional tradition to enact laws of this sort. Central both to the idea of the rule of law and to our own Constitution's guarantee of equal protection is the principle that government and each of its parts remain open on impartial terms to all who seek its assistance. . . . Respect for this principle explains why laws singling out a certain class of citizens for disfavored legal status or general hardships are rare. A law declaring that in general it shall be more difficult for one group of citizens than for all others to seek aid from the government is itself a denial of equal protection of the laws in the most literal sense. . . .

The primary rationale the State offers for Amendment 2 is respect for other citizens' freedom of association, and in particular the liberties of landlords or employers who have personal or religious objections to homosexuality. Colorado also cites its interest in conserving resources to fight discrimination against other groups. The breadth of the Amendment is so far removed from these particular justifications that we find it impossible to credit them. We cannot say that Amendment 2 is directed to any identifiable legitimate purpose or discrete objective. It is a status-based enactment divorced from any factual context from which we could discern a relationship to legitimate state interests; it is a classification of persons undertaken for its own sake, something the Equal Protection Clause does not permit.

We must conclude that Amendment 2 classifies homosexuals not to further a proper legislative end but to make them unequal to everyone else. This Colorado cannot do. A State cannot so deem a class of persons a stranger to its laws. Amendment 2 violates the Equal Protection Clause, and the judgment of the Supreme Court of Colorado is affirmed.

It is so ordered.

Lawrence v. Texas (2003)

In this landmark case, the Supreme Court ruled that laws restricting private gay sex were unconstitutional. This case extended findings from Roe v. Wade *and* Griswold v. Connecticut *about the right to privacy. It also reversed* Bowers.

JUSTICE KENNEDY delivered the opinion of the Court.

Liberty protects the person from unwarranted government intrusions into a dwelling or other private places. In our tradition the State is not omnipresent in the home. And there are other spheres of our lives and existence, outside the home, where the State should not be a dominant presence. Freedom extends beyond spatial bounds. Liberty presumes an autonomy of self that includes freedom of thought, belief, expression, and certain intimate conduct. The instant case involves liberty of the person both in its spatial and more transcendent dimensions.

I

The question before the Court is the validity of a Texas statute making it a crime for two persons of the same sex to engage in certain intimate sexual conduct.

In Houston, Texas, officers of the Harris county Police Department were dispatched to a private residence in response to a reported weapons disturbance. They entered an apartment where one of the petitioners, John Geddes Lawrence, resided. The right of the police to enter does not seem to have been questioned. The officers observed Lawrence and another man, Tyron Garner, engaging in a sexual act. The two petitioners were arrested, held in custody over night, and charged and convicted before a Justice of the Peace. . . .

We granted certiorari to consider . . .

> "1. Whether Petitioners' criminal convictions under the Texas 'Homosexual Conduct' law—which criminalizes sexual intimacy by same-sex couples, but not identical behavior by different-sex couples—violate the Fourteenth Amendment guarantee of equal protection of laws?
>
> "2. Whether Petitioners' criminal convictions for adult consensual sexual intimacy in the home violate their vital interests in liberty and privacy protected by the Due Process Clause of the Fourteenth Amendment?" . . .

The petitioners were adults at the time of the alleged offense. Their conduct was in private and consensual.

II

We conclude the case should be resolved by determining whether the petitioners were free as adults to engage in the private conduct in the exercise of their liberty under the Due Process Clause of the Fourteenth Amendment to the Constitution. . . .

. . . When homosexual conduct is made criminal by the law of the State, that declaration in and of itself is an invitation to subject homosexual persons to discrimination both in the public and in the private spheres. . . .

The stigma this criminal statute imposes, moreover, is not trivial. The offense, to be sure, is but a class C misdemeanor, a minor offense in the Texas legal system. Still, it remains a criminal offense with all that imports for the dignity of the persons charged. The petitioners will bear on their record the history of their criminal convictions. . . .

Furthermore, the Texas criminal conviction carries with it the other collateral consequences always following a conviction, such as notations on job application forms, to mention but one example. . . .

The present case does not involve minors. It does not involve persons who might be injured or coerced or who are situated in relationships where consent might not easily be refused. It does not involve public conduct or prostitution. It does not involve whether the government must give formal recognition to any relationship that homosexual persons seek to enter. The case does involve two adults who, with full and mutual consent from each other, engaged in sexual practices common to a homosexual lifestyle. The petitioners are entitled to respect for their private lives. The State cannot demean their existence or control their destiny by making their private sexual conduct a crime. Their right to liberty under the Due Process Clause gives them the full right to engage in their conduct without intervention of the government. . . . The Texas statute furthers no legitimate state interest which can justify its intrusion into the personal and private life of the individual.

Had those who drew and ratified the Due Process Clauses of the Fifth Amendment or the Fourteenth Amendment known the components of liberty in its manifold possibilities, they might have been more specific. They did not presume to have this insight. They knew times can blind us to certain truths and later generations can see that laws once thought necessary and proper in fact serve only to oppress. As the Constitution endures, persons in every generation can invoke its principles in their own search for greater freedom.

The judgment of the Court of Appeals for the Texas Fourteenth District is reversed, and the case is remanded for further proceedings not inconsistent with this opinion.

It is so ordered.

Obergefell v. Hodges
(2015)

This landmark case legalized same-sex marriages in the United States and asserted that such unions received protection directly from the Constitution.

JUSTICE KENNEDY delivered the opinion of the Court.

The Constitution promises liberty to all within its reach, a liberty that includes certain specific rights that allow persons, within a lawful realm, to define and express their identity. The petitioners in these cases seek to find that liberty by marrying someone of the same sex and having their marriages deemed lawful on the same terms and conditions as marriages between persons of the opposite sex.

I

These cases come from Michigan, Kentucky, Ohio, and Tennessee, States that define marriage as a union between one man and one woman. . . .

The petitioners sought certiorari. This Court granted review, limited to two questions. The first, presented by the cases from Michigan and Kentucky, is whether the Fourteenth Amendment requires a State to license a marriage between two people of the same sex. The second, presented by the cases from Ohio, Tennessee, and, again, Kentucky, is whether the Fourteenth Amendment requires a State to recognize a same-sex marriage licensed and performed in a State which does grant that right. . . .

From their beginning to their most recent page, the annals of human history reveal the transcendent importance of marriage. The lifelong union of a man and a woman always has promised nobility and dignity to all persons, without regard to their station in life. Marriage is sacred to those who live by their religions and offers unique fulfillment to those who find meaning in the secular realm. Its dynamic allows two people to find a life that could not be found alone, for a marriage becomes greater than just the two persons. Rising from the most basic human needs, marriage is essential to our most profound hopes and aspirations.

The centrality of marriage to the human condition makes it unsurprising that the institution has existed for millennia and across civilizations. . . . There are untold references to the beauty of marriage in religious and philosophical texts spanning time, cultures, and faiths, as well as in art and literature in all their forms. It is fair and necessary to say these references were based on the understanding that marriage is a union between two persons of the opposite sex.

That history is the beginning of these cases. The respondents say it should be the end as well. To them, it would demean a timeless institution if the concept and lawful status of marriage were extended to two persons of the same sex. Marriage, in their view, is by its nature a gender-differentiated union of man and woman. This view long has been held and continues to be held in good faith by reasonable and sincere people here and throughout the world.

The petitioners acknowledge this history but contend that these cases cannot end there. Were their intent to demean the revered idea and reality of marriage, the petitioners' claims would be of a different order. But that is neither their purpose nor their submission. To the contrary, it is the enduring importance of marriage that underlies the petitioners' contentions. This, they say, is their whole point. Far from seeking to devalue marriage, the petitioners seek it for themselves because of their respect and need for its privileges and responsibilities. And their immutable nature dictates that same-sex marriage is their only real path to this profound commitment.

Recounting the circumstances of three of these cases illustrates the urgency of the petitioners' cause from their perspective. Petitioner James Obergefell, a plaintiff in the Ohio case, met John Arthur over two decades ago. They fell in love and started a life together, establishing a lasting, committed relation. In 2011, however, Arthur was diagnosed with amyotrophic lateral sclerosis, or ALS. This debilitating disease is progressive, with no known cure. Two years ago, Obergefell and Arthur decided to commit to one another, resolving to marry before Arthur died. To fulfill their mutual promise, they traveled from Ohio to Maryland, where same-sex marriage was legal. It was difficult for Arthur to move, and so the couple were wed inside a medical transport plane as it remained on the tarmac in Baltimore. Three months later, Arthur died. Ohio law does not permit Obergefell to be listed as the surviving spouse on Arthur's death certificate. By statute, they must remain strangers even in death, a state-imposed separation Obergefell deems "hurtful for the rest of time." He brought suit to be shown as the surviving spouse on Arthur's death certificate. . . .

The cases now before the Court involve other petitioners as well, each with their own experiences. Their stories reveal that they seek not to denigrate marriage but rather to live their lives, or honor their spouses' memory, joined by its bond. . . .

III

Under the Due Process Clause of the Fourteenth Amendment, no State shall "deprive any person of life, liberty, or property, without due process of law." The fundamental liberties protected by this Clause include most of the rights enumerated in the Bill of Rights. In addition these liberties extend to certain personal choices central to individual dignity and autonomy, including intimate choices that define personal identity and beliefs.

The identification and protection of fundamental rights is an enduring part of the judicial duty to interpret the Constitution. . . .

The nature of injustice is that we may not always see it in our own times. The generations that wrote and ratified the Bill of Rights and the Fourteenth Amendment did not presume to know the extent of freedom in all of its dimensions, and so they entrusted to future generations a charter protecting the right of all persons to enjoy liberty as we learn its meaning. When new insight reveals discord between the Constitution's central protections and a received legal stricture, a claim to liberty must be addressed.

Applying these established tenets, the Court has long held the right to marry is protected by the Constitution. . . .

Over time and in other contexts, the Court has reiterated that the right to marry is fundamental under the Due Process Clause.

It cannot be denied that this Court's cases describing the right to marry presumed a relationship involving opposite-sex partners. The Court, like many institutions, has made assumptions defined by the world and time of which it is a part. . . .

Still, there are other, more instructive precedents. This Court's cases have expressed constitutional principles of broader reach. In defining the right to marry these cases have identified essential attributes of that right based in history, tradition, and other constitutional liberties inherent in this intimate bond. And in assessing whether the force and rationale of its cases apply to same-sex couples, the Court must respect the basic reasons why the right to marry has been long protected.

This analysis compels the conclusion that same-sex couples may exercise the right to marry. The four principles and traditions to be discussed demonstrate that the reasons marriage is fundamental under the Constitution apply with equal force to same-sex couples.

A first premise of the Court's relevant precedents is that the right to personal choice regarding marriage is inherent in the concept of individual autonomy. . . .

The nature of marriage is that, through its enduring bond, two persons together can find other freedoms, such as expression, intimacy, and spirituality. This is true for all persons, whatever their sexual orientation. There is dignity in the bond between two men or two women who seek to marry and in their autonomy to make such profound choices. . . .

A second principle in this Court's jurisprudence is that the right to marry is fundamental because it supports a two-person union unlike any other in its importance to the committed individuals. . . .

. . . Marriage responds to the universal fear that a lonely person might call out only to find no one there. It offers the hope of companionship and understanding and assurance that while both still live there will be someone to care for the other. . . .

A third basis for protecting the right to marry is that it safeguards children and families and thus draws meaning from related rights of childrearing, procreation, and education. . . .

Fourth and finally, this Court's cases and the Nation's traditions make clear that marriage is a keystone of our social order. . . .

For that reason, just as a couple vows to support each other, so does society pledge to support the couple, offering symbolic recognition and material benefits to protect and nourish the union. Indeed, while the States are in general free to vary the benefits they confer on all married couples, they have throughout our history made marriage the basis for an expanding list of governmental rights, benefits, and responsibilities. These aspects of marital status include: taxation; inheritance and property rights; rules of intestate succession; spousal privilege in the law of evidence; hospital access; medical decisionmaking authority; adoption rights; the rights and benefits of survivors; birth and death certificates; professional ethics rules; campaign finance restrictions; workers' compensation benefits; health insurance; and child custody, support, and visitation rules. . . . The States have contributed to the fundamental character of the marriage right by placing that institution at the center of so many facets of the legal and social order.

There is no difference between same- and opposite-sex couples with respect to this principle. Yet by virtue of their exclusion from that institution, same-sex couples are denied the constellation of benefits that the States have linked to marriage. This harm results in more than just material burdens. Same-sex couples are consigned to an instability many opposite-sex couples would deem intolerable in their own lives. As the State itself makes marriage all the more precious by the significance it attaches to it, exclusion from that status has the effect of teaching that gays and lesbians are unequal in important respects. It demeans gays and lesbians for the State to lock them out of a central institution of the Nation's society. Same-sex couples, too, may aspire to the transcendent purposes of marriage and seek fulfillment in its highest meaning.

The limitation of marriage to opposite-sex couples may long have seemed natural and just, but its inconsistency with the central meaning of the fundamental right to marry is now manifest. With that knowledge must come the recognition that laws excluding same-sex couples from the marriage right impose stigma and injury of the kind prohibited by our basic charter. . . .

V

These cases also present the question whether the Constitution requires States to recognize same-sex marriages validly performed out of State. As made clear by the case of Obergefell and Arthur, and by that of DeKoe and Kostura, the recognition bans inflict substantial and continuing harm on same-sex couples. . . .

. . . The Court, in this decision, holds same-sex couples may exercise the fundamental right to marry in all States. It follows that the Court also must hold and it now does hold that there is no lawful basis for a State to refuse to recognize a lawful same-sex marriage performed in another State on the ground of its same-sex character.

No union is more profound than marriage, for it embodies the highest ideals of love, fidelity, devotion, sacrifice, and family. In forming a marital union, two people become something greater than once they were. As some of the petitioners in these cases demonstrate, marriage embodies a love that may endure even past death. It would misunderstand these men and women to say they disrespect the idea of marriage. Their plea is that they do respect it, respect it so deeply that they seek to find its fulfillment for themselves. Their hope is not to be condemned to live in loneliness, excluded from one of civilization's oldest institutions. They ask for equal dignity in the eyes of the law. The Constitution grants them that right.

The judgment of the Court of Appeals for the Sixth Circuit is reversed.

It is so ordered.

Part VI

ELECTORAL PROCESSES

———— ☆ ————

Our final part deals with the extent to which the Constitution protects rights to free and fair elections. As with the other controversies we have covered, this one remains a source of contention among the justices and the American people. The cases here examine issues such as the right to have one's vote counted equally, the right of corporations to engage in election speech, and whether race can be a factor in drawing legislative districts. The right to vote is central to the very existence of self-government. Readers of these cases think for themselves about the proper role of the Supreme Court in policing this essential part of our political process.

Baker v. Carr
(1961)

> *Because legislative apportionment, or the process of allo-
> cating seats to determine political representation, deals
> with a political problem, the Supreme Court might have
> lacked jurisdiction to make decisions in disputes over it.
> But in this case, the Supreme Court explains why it does
> have the legal jurisdiction to weigh in.*

MR. JUSTICE BRENNAN delivered the opinion of the
Court.

This civil action was brought under 42 U.S.C. §§ 1983
and 1988 to redress the alleged deprivation of federal constitutional rights. The complaint, alleging that, by means of a
1901 statute of Tennessee apportioning the members of the
General Assembly among the State's 95 counties, "these
plaintiffs and others similarly situated, are denied the equal
protection of the laws accorded them by the Fourteenth
Amendment to the Constitution of the United States by virtue of the debasement of their votes," was dismissed by a
three-judge court convened under 28 U.S.C. § 2281 in the
Middle District of Tennessee.... We hold that the dismissal

was error, and remand the cause to the District Court for trial and further proceedings consistent with this opinion.

The General Assembly of Tennessee consists of the Senate, with 33 members, and the House of Representatives, with 99 members. . . .

. . . Tennessee's standard for allocating legislative representation among her counties is the total number of qualified voters resident in the respective counties, subject only to minor qualifications. Decennial reapportionment in compliance with the constitutional scheme was effected by the General Assembly each decade from 1871 to 1901. The 1871 apportionment was preceded by an 1870 statute requiring an enumeration. . . . In 1901, the General Assembly abandoned separate enumeration in favor of reliance upon the Federal Census, and passed the Apportionment Act here in controversy. In the more than 60 years since that action, all proposals in both Houses of the General Assembly for reapportionment have failed to pass.

Between 1901 and 1961, Tennessee has experienced substantial growth and redistribution of her population. In 1901, the population was 2,020,616, of whom 487,380 were eligible to vote. The 1960 Federal Census reports the State's population at 3,567,089, of whom 2,092,891 are eligible to vote. The relative standings of the counties in terms of qualified voters have changed significantly. It is primarily the continued application of the 1901 Apportionment Act to this shifted and enlarged voting population which gives rise to the present controversy.

Indeed, the complaint alleges that the 1901 statute, even as of the time of its passage,

> "made no apportionment of Representatives and Senators in accordance with the constitutional formula . . . , but instead arbitrarily and capriciously apportioned

representatives in the Senate and House without reference . . . to any logical or reasonable formula whatever."

It is further alleged that, "because of the population changes since 1900, and the failure of the Legislature to reapportion itself since 1901," the 1901 statute became "unconstitutional and obsolete." Appellants also argue that, because of the composition of the legislature effected by the 1901 Apportionment Act, redress in the form of a state constitutional amendment to change the entire mechanism for reapportioning, or any other change short of that, is difficult or impossible. . . .

IV

JUSTICIABILITY

In holding that the subject matter of this suit was not justiciable, the District Court relied on *Colegrove v. Green* and subsequent per curiam cases. The court stated:

"From a review of these decisions, there can be no doubt that the federal rule . . . is that the federal courts . . . will not intervene in cases of this type to compel legislative reapportionment."

We understand the District Court to have read the cited cases as compelling the conclusion that, since the appellants sought to have a legislative apportionment held unconstitutional, their suit presented a "political question," and was therefore nonjusticiable. We hold that this challenge to an apportionment presents no nonjusticiable "political question." The cited cases do not hold the contrary.

Of course, the mere fact that the suit seeks protection of a political right does not mean it presents a political question. . . . Rather, it is argued that apportionment cases, whatever the actual wording of the complaint, can involve no federal constitutional right except one resting on the guaranty of a republican form of government, and that complaints based on that clause have been held to present political questions which are nonjusticiable.

We hold that the claim pleaded here neither rests upon nor implicates the Guaranty Clause, and that its justiciability is therefore not foreclosed by our decisions of cases involving that clause. The District Court misinterpreted *Colegrove v. Green* and other decisions of this Court on which it relied. . . .

. . . But because there appears to be some uncertainty as to why those cases did present political questions, and specifically as to whether this apportionment case is like those cases, we deem it necessary first to consider the contours of the "political question" doctrine.

Our discussion, even at the price of extending this opinion, requires review of a number of political question cases, in order to expose the attributes of the doctrine—attributes which, in various settings, diverge, combine, appear, and disappear in seeming disorderliness. Since that review is undertaken solely to demonstrate that neither singly nor collectively do these cases support a conclusion that this apportionment case is nonjusticiable, we, of course, do not explore their implications in other contexts. That review reveals that, in the Guaranty Clause cases and in the other "political question" cases, it is the relationship between the judiciary and the coordinate branches of the Federal Government, and not the federal judiciary's relationship to the States, which gives rise to the "political question." . . .

The nonjusticiability of a political question is primarily a function of the separation of powers. . . .

Foreign relations: there are sweeping statements to the effect that all questions touching foreign relations are political questions. Not only does resolution of such issues frequently turn on standards that defy judicial application, or involve the exercise of a discretion demonstrably committed to the executive or legislature, but many such questions uniquely demand single-voiced statement of the Government's views. Yet it is error to suppose that every case or controversy which touches foreign relations lies beyond judicial cognizance. . . . For example, though a court will not ordinarily inquire whether a treaty has been terminated, since on that question, "governmental action . . . must be regarded as of controlling importance," if there has been no conclusive "governmental action," then a court can construe a treaty, and may find it provides the answer. . . .

While recognition of foreign governments so strongly defies judicial treatment that, without executive recognition, a foreign state has been called "a republic of whose existence we know nothing," and the judiciary ordinarily follows the executive as to which nation has sovereignty over disputed territory, once sovereignty over an area is politically determined and declared, courts may examine the resulting status and decide independently whether a statute applies to that area. Similarly, recognition of belligerency abroad is an executive responsibility, but if the executive proclamations fall short of an explicit answer, a court may construe them seeking, for example, to determine whether the situation is such that statutes designed to assure American neutrality have become operative. . . .

Dates of duration of hostilities: though it has been stated broadly that "the power which declared the necessity is the power to declare its cessation, and what the cessation requires," here too analysis reveals isolable reasons for the presence of political questions, underlying this Court's refusal to review the political departments' determination of when or whether a war has ended. . . . But deference rests on reason, not habit. The question in a particular case may not seriously implicate considerations of finality—*e.g.*, a public program of importance (rent control), yet not central to the emergency effort. Further, clearly definable criteria for decision may be available. In such case, the political question barrier falls away. . . .

Validity of enactments: in *Coleman v. Miller*, this Court held that the questions of how long a proposed amendment to the Federal Constitution remained open to ratification, and what effect a prior rejection had on a subsequent ratification, were committed to congressional resolution and involved criteria of decision that necessarily escaped the judicial grasp. Similar considerations apply to the enacting process. . . .

The status of Indian tribes: this Court's deference to the political departments in determining whether Indians are recognized as a tribe, while it reflects familiar attributes of political questions, also has a unique element . . .

. . . Able to discern what is "distinctly Indian," the courts will strike down any heedless extension of that label. They will not stand impotent before an obvious instance of a manifestly unauthorized exercise of power.

It is apparent that several formulations which vary slightly according to the settings in which the questions arise may describe a political question, although each has one or more elements which identify it as essentially a function of the separation of powers. Prominent on the surface of any case held to involve a political question is found a textually demonstrable constitutional commitment of the issue to a coordinate political department; or a lack of judicially discoverable and manageable standards for resolving it; or the impossibility of deciding without an initial policy determination of a kind clearly for nonjudicial discretion; or the impossibility of a court's undertaking independent resolution without expressing lack of the respect due coordinate branches of government; or an unusual need for unquestioning adherence to a political decision already made; or the potentiality of embarrassment from multifarious pronouncements by various departments on one question.

. . . The doctrine of which we treat is one of "political questions," not one of "political cases." . . .

But it is argued that this case shares the characteristics of decisions that constitute a category not yet considered, cases concerning the Constitution's guaranty, in Art. IV, § 4, of a republican form of government. A conclusion as to whether the case at bar does present a political question cannot be confidently reached until we have considered those cases with special care. We shall discover that Guaranty Clause claims involve those elements which define a "political question," and, for that reason and no other, they are nonjusticiable. In particular, we shall discover that the nonjusticiability of such claims has nothing to do with their touching upon matters of state governmental organization. . . .

We come, finally, to the ultimate inquiry whether our precedents as to what constitutes a nonjusticiable "political question" bring the case before us under the umbrella of that doctrine. A natural beginning is to note whether any of the common characteristics which we have been able to identify and label descriptively are present. We find none: the question here is the consistency of state action with the Federal

Constitution. We have no question decided, or to be decided, by a political branch of government coequal with this Court. Nor do we risk embarrassment of our government abroad, or grave disturbance at home if we take issue with Tennessee as to the constitutionality of her action here challenged. Nor need the appellants, in order to succeed in this action, ask the Court to enter upon policy determinations for which judicially manageable standards are lacking. Judicial standards under the Equal Protection Clause are well developed and familiar, and it has been open to courts since the enactment of the Fourteenth Amendment to determine, if, on the particular facts, they must, that a discrimination reflects no policy, but simply arbitrary and capricious action. . . .

We conclude that the complaint's allegations of a denial of equal protection present a justiciable constitutional cause of action upon which appellants are entitled to a trial and a decision. The right asserted is within the reach of judicial protection under the Fourteenth Amendment.

The judgment of the District Court is reversed, and the cause is remanded for further proceedings consistent with this opinion.

Reversed and remanded.

Reynolds v. Sims
(1964)

> *This case furthered the principle of "one person, one vote."*
> *The Supreme Court ruled that electoral districts repre-*
> *sented by state legislative chambers must be roughly*
> *equal in population.*

MR. CHIEF JUSTICE WARREN delivered the opinion of the Court.

Involved in these cases are an appeal and two cross-appeals from a decision of the Federal District Court for the Middle District of Alabama holding invalid, under the Equal Protection Clause of the Federal Constitution, the existing and two legislatively proposed plans for the apportionment of seats in the two houses of the Alabama Legislature, and ordering into effect a temporary reapportionment plan comprised of parts of the proposed but judicially disapproved measures.

I

On August 26, 1961, the original plaintiffs, residents, tax-payers and voters of Jefferson County, Alabama, filed a complaint in the United States District Court for the Middle District of Alabama, in their own behalf and on behalf of all similarly situated Alabama voters, challenging the apportionment of the Alabama Legislature. . . .

The complaint stated that the Alabama Legislature was composed of a Senate of 35 members and a House of Representatives of 106 members. . . .

The maximum size of the Alabama House was increased from 105 to 106 with the creation of a new county in 1903, pursuant to the constitutional provision which states that, in addition to the prescribed 105 House seats, each county thereafter created shall be entitled to one representative. . . .

Plaintiffs below alleged that the last apportionment of the Alabama Legislature was based on the 1900 federal census, despite the requirement of the State Constitution that the legislature be reapportioned decennially. They asserted that, since the population growth in the State from 1900 to 1960 had been uneven, Jefferson and other counties were now victims of serious discrimination with respect to the allocation of legislative representation. As a result of the failure of the legislature to reapportion itself, plaintiffs asserted, they were denied "equal suffrage in free and equal elections . . . and the equal protection of the laws," in violation of the Alabama Constitution and the Fourteenth Amendment to the Federal Constitution. The complaint asserted that plaintiffs had no other adequate remedy, and that they had exhausted all forms of relief other than that available through the federal courts. . . .

On July 12, 1962, an extraordinary session of the Alabama Legislature adopted two reapportionment plans to take effect for the 1966 elections. One was a proposed constitutional amendment, referred to as the "67-Senator Amendment." It provided for a House of Representatives consisting of 106 members, apportioned by giving one seat to each of Alabama's 67 counties and distributing the others according to population by the "equal proportions" method. Using this formula, the constitutional amendment specified the number of representatives allotted to each county until a new apportionment could be made on the basis of the 1970 census. The Senate was to be composed of 67 members, one from each county. The legislation provided that the proposed amendment should be submitted to the voters for ratification at the November 1962 general election.

The other reapportionment plan was embodied in a statutory measure adopted by the legislature and signed into law by the Alabama Governor, and was referred to as the "Crawford-Webb Act." It was enacted as standby legislation, to take effect in 1966 if the proposed constitutional amendment should fail of passage by a majority of the State's voters, or should the federal courts refuse to accept the proposed amendment (though not rejected by the voters) as effective action in compliance with the requirements of the Fourteenth Amendment. The act provided for a Senate consisting of 35 members, representing 35 senatorial districts established along county lines, and altered only a few of the former districts. In apportioning the 106 seats in the Alabama House of Representatives, the statutory measure gave each county one seat, and apportioned the remaining 39 on a rough population basis, under a formula requiring increasingly more population for a county to be accorded additional seats. . . .

The evidence adduced at trial before the three-judge panel consisted primarily of figures showing the population of each Alabama county and senatorial district according to the 1960 census, and the number of representatives allocated to each county under each of the three plans at issue in the litigation—the existing apportionment (under the 1901 constitutional provisions and the current statutory measures substantially reenacting the same plan), the proposed 67-Senator constitutional amendment, and the Crawford-Webb Act. Under all three plans, each senatorial district would be represented by only one senator.

On July 21, 1962, the District Court held that the inequality of the existing representation in the Alabama Legislature violated the Equal Protection Clause of the Fourteenth Amendment. . . . Under the existing provisions, applying 1960 census figures, only 25.1% of the State's total population resided in districts represented by a majority of the members of the Senate, and only 25.7% lived in counties which could elect a majority of the members of the House of Representatives. . . .

The Court then considered both the proposed constitutional amendment and the Crawford-Webb Act to ascertain whether the legislature had taken effective action to remedy the unconstitutional aspects of the existing apportionment. In initially summarizing the result which it had reached, the Court stated:

> "This Court has reached the conclusion that neither the '67-Senator Amendment' nor the 'Crawford-Webb Act' meets the necessary constitutional requirements. We find that each of the legislative acts, when considered as a whole, is so obviously discriminatory, arbitrary and irrational . . ."

II

Undeniably, the Constitution of the United States protects the right of all qualified citizens to vote, in state as well as in federal, elections. A consistent line of decisions by this Court in cases involving attempts to deny or restrict the right of suffrage has made this indelibly clear. It has been repeatedly recognized that all qualified voters have a constitutionally protected right to vote and to have their votes counted. . . . The right to vote freely for the candidate of one's choice is of the essence of a democratic society, and any restrictions on that right strike at the heart of representative government. And the right of suffrage can be denied by a debasement or dilution of the weight of a citizen's vote just as effectively as by wholly prohibiting the free exercise of the franchise.

In *Baker v. Carr*, we held that a claim asserted under the Equal Protection Clause challenging the constitutionality of a State's apportionment of seats in its legislature, on the ground that the right to vote of certain citizens was effectively impaired, since debased and diluted, in effect presented a justiciable controversy subject to adjudication by federal courts. . . .

III

A predominant consideration in determining whether a State's legislative apportionment scheme constitutes an invidious discrimination violative of rights asserted under the Equal Protection Clause is that the rights allegedly impaired are individual and personal in nature. . . .

Legislators represent people, not trees or acres. Legislators are elected by voters, not farms or cities or economic interests. As long as ours is a representative form of government, and our legislatures are those instruments of government elected directly by and directly representative of the people, the right to elect legislators in a free and unimpaired fashion is a bedrock of our political system. It could hardly be gainsaid that a constitutional claim had been asserted by an allegation that certain otherwise qualified voters had been entirely prohibited from voting for members of their state legislature. And, if a State should provide that the votes of citizens in one part of the State should be given two times, or five times, or 10 times the weight of votes of citizens in another part of the State, it could hardly be contended that the right to vote of those residing in the disfavored areas had not been effectively diluted. It would appear extraordinary to suggest that a State could be constitutionally permitted to enact a law providing that certain of the State's voters could vote two, five, or 10 times for their legislative representatives, while voters living elsewhere could vote only once. And it is inconceivable that a state law to the effect that, in counting votes for legislators, the votes of citizens in one part of the State would be multiplied by two, five, or 10, while the votes of persons in another area would be counted only at face value, could be constitutionally sustainable. Of course, the effect of state legislative districting schemes which give the same number of representatives to unequal numbers of constituents is identical. Overweighting and overvaluation of the votes of those living here has the certain effect of dilution and undervaluation of the votes of those living there. The resulting discrimination against those individual voters living in disfavored areas is easily demonstrable mathematically. Their right to vote is simply not the same right to vote as that of those living in a favored part of the State. Two, five, or 10 of them must vote before the effect of their voting is equivalent to that of their favored neighbor. Weighting the votes of citizens differently, by any method or means, merely because of where they happen to reside, hardly seems justifiable. . . .

State legislatures are, historically, the fountainhead of representative government in this country. . . . Full and effective participation by all citizens in state government requires, therefore, that each citizen have an equally effective voice in the election of members of his state legislature. Modern and viable state government needs, and the Constitution demands, no less.

. . . Since the achieving of fair and effective representation for all citizens is concededly the basic aim of legislative apportionment, we conclude that the Equal Protection Clause guarantees the opportunity for equal participation by all voters in the election of state legislators. Diluting the weight of votes because of place of residence impairs basic constitutional rights under the Fourteenth Amendment just as much as invidious discriminations based upon factors such as race or economic status. . . .

IV

We hold that, as a basic constitutional standard, the Equal Protection Clause requires that the seats in both houses of a bicameral state legislature must be apportioned on a population basis. Simply stated, an individual's right to vote for state legislators is unconstitutionally impaired when its weight is in a substantial fashion diluted when compared with votes of citizens living in other parts of the State. Since under neither the existing apportionment provisions nor either of the

proposed plans was either of the houses of the Alabama Legislature apportioned on a population basis, the District Court
correctly held that all three of these schemes were constitutionally invalid. Furthermore, the existing apportionment,
and also, to a lesser extent, the apportionment under the
Crawford-Webb Act, presented little more than crazy quilts,
completely lacking in rationality, and could be found invalid
on that basis alone. . . .

VI

By holding that, as a federal constitutional requisite, both
houses of a state legislature must be apportioned on a population basis, we mean that the Equal Protection Clause requires that a State make an honest and good faith effort to
construct districts, in both houses of its legislature, as nearly
of equal population as is practicable. . . .

Shaw v. Reno
(1993)

> *In this case, the Supreme Court found that North Carolina's efforts to create a racially gerrymandered district violated the Fourteenth Amendment's Equal Protection Clause.*

JUSTICE O'CONNOR delivered the opinion of the Court.

This case involves two of the most complex and sensitive issues this Court has faced in recent years: the meaning of the constitutional "right" to vote, and the propriety of race-based state legislation designed to benefit members of historically disadvantaged racial minority groups. As a result of the 1990 census, North Carolina became entitled to a 12th seat in the United States House of Representatives. The General Assembly enacted a reapportionment plan that included one majority-black congressional district. After the Attorney General of the United States objected to the plan pursuant to §5 of the Voting Rights Act of 1965, the General Assembly passed new legislation creating a second majority-black district. Appellants allege that the revised plan, which contains district boundary lines of dramatically irregular shape, constitutes an unconstitutional racial gerrymander. The question before us is whether appellants have stated a cognizable claim. . . .

II

A

"The right to vote freely for the candidate of one's choice is of the essence of a democratic society. . . ." For much of our Nation's history, that right sadly has been denied to many because of race. The Fifteenth Amendment, ratified in 1870 after a bloody Civil War, promised unequivocally that "[t]he right of citizens of the United States to vote" no longer would be "denied or abridged . . . by any State on account of race, color, or previous condition of servitude."

But "[a] number of states . . . refused to take no for an answer and continued to circumvent the fifteenth amendment's prohibition through the use of both subtle and blunt instruments, perpetuating ugly patterns of pervasive racial discrimination." Ostensibly race-neutral devices such as literacy tests with "grandfather" clauses and "good character" provisos were devised to deprive black voters of the franchise.

Another of the weapons in the States' arsenal was the racial gerrymander—"the deliberate and arbitrary distortion of district boundaries . . . for [racial] purposes." . . .

But it soon became apparent that guaranteeing equal access to the polls would not suffice to root out other racially discriminatory voting practices. Drawing on the "one person, one vote" principle, this Court recognized that "[t]he right to vote can be affected by a dilution of voting power as well as by an absolute prohibition on casting a ballot." . . .

B

It is against this background that we confront the questions presented here. . . . Our focus is on appellants' claim that the State engaged in unconstitutional racial gerrymandering. That argument strikes a powerful historical chord: it is unsettling how closely the North Carolina plan resembles the most egregious racial gerrymanders of the past.

An understanding of the nature of appellants' claim is critical to our resolution of the case. In their complaint, appellants did not claim that the General Assembly's reapportionment plan unconstitutionally "diluted" white voting strength. They did not even claim to be white. Rather, appellants' complaint alleged that the deliberate segregation of voters into separate districts on the basis of race violated their constitutional right to participate in a "color-blind" electoral process.

Despite their invocation of the ideal of a "color-blind" Constitution, appellants appear to concede that race-conscious redistricting is not always unconstitutional. That concession is wise: this Court never has held that race-conscious state decisionmaking is impermissible in *all* circumstances. What appellants object to is redistricting legislation that is so extremely irregular on its face that it rationally can be viewed only as an effort to segregate the races for purposes of voting, without regard for traditional districting principles and without sufficiently compelling justification. For the reasons that follow, we conclude that appellants have stated a claim upon which relief can be granted under the Equal Protection Clause. . . .

III

. . . In some exceptional cases, a reapportionment plan may be so highly irregular that, on its face, it rationally cannot be understood as anything other than an effort to "segregat[e] . . . voters" on the basis of race. . . . So, too, would be a case in which a State concentrated a dispersed minority population in a single district by disregarding traditional districting principles such as compactness, contiguity, and respect for political subdivisions. We emphasize that these criteria are important not because they are constitutionally required— they are not—but because they are objective factors that may serve to defeat a claim that a district has been gerrymandered on racial lines.

Put differently, we believe that reapportionment is one area in which appearances do matter. A reapportionment plan that includes in one district individuals who belong to the same race, but who are otherwise widely separated by geographical and political boundaries, and who may have little in common with one another but the color of their skin, bears an uncomfortable resemblance to political apartheid. It reinforces the perception that members of the same racial group—regardless of their age, education, economic status, or the community in which they live—think alike, share the same political interests, and will prefer the same candidates at the polls. We have rejected such perceptions elsewhere as impermissible racial stereotypes. . . . By perpetuating such notions, a racial gerrymander may exacerbate the very patterns of racial bloc voting that majority-minority districting is sometimes said to counteract.

The message that such districting sends to elected representatives is equally pernicious. When a district obviously is created solely to effectuate the perceived common interests of one racial group, elected officials are more likely to believe that their primary obligation is to represent only the members of that group, rather than their constituency as a whole. This is altogether antithetical to our system of representative democracy. . . .

For these reasons, we conclude that a plaintiff challenging a reapportionment statute under the Equal Protection Clause may state a claim by alleging that the legislation, though race neutral on its face, rationally cannot be understood as anything other than an effort to separate voters into different districts on the basis of race, and that the separation lacks sufficient justification. . . .

V

Racial classifications of any sort pose the risk of lasting harm to our society. They reinforce the belief, held by too many for too much of our history, that individuals should be judged by the color of their skin. Racial classifications with respect to voting carry particular dangers. Racial gerrymandering, even for remedial purposes, may balkanize us into competing racial factions; it threatens to carry us further from the goal of a political system in which race no longer matters—a goal that the Fourteenth and Fifteenth Amendments embody, and to which the Nation continues to aspire. It is for these reasons that race-based districting by our state legislatures demands close judicial scrutiny.

In this case, the Attorney General suggested that North Carolina could have created a reasonably compact second majority-minority district in the south-central to southeastern part of the State. . . . Today we hold only that appellants have stated a claim under the Equal Protection Clause by alleging that the North Carolina General Assembly adopted a reapportionment scheme so irrational on its face that it can be understood only as an effort to segregate voters into separate voting districts because of their race, and that the separation lacks sufficient justification. If the allegation of racial gerrymandering remains uncontradicted, the District Court further must determine whether the North Carolina plan is narrowly tailored to further a compelling governmental interest. Accordingly, we reverse the judgment of the District Court and remand the case for further proceedings consistent with this opinion.

It is so ordered.

Citizens United v. Federal Election Commission (2010)

> *In this landmark case, the Supreme Court protected corporate funding of advertisements that endorsed candidates during elections. The Court also held that corporations have free speech rights protected by the First Amendment, a decision that would have wide-reaching implications for money in politics.*

JUSTICE KENNEDY delivered the opinion of the Court.

Federal law prohibits corporations and unions from using their general treasury funds to make independent expenditures for speech defined as an "electioneering communication" or for speech expressly advocating the election or defeat of a candidate. Limits on electioneering communications were upheld in *McConnell v. Federal Election Comm'n* (2003). The holding of *McConnell* rested to a large extent on an earlier case, *Austin v. Michigan Chamber of Commerce* (1990). *Austin* had held that political speech may be banned based on the speaker's corporate identity.

In this case we are asked to reconsider *Austin* and, in effect, *McConnell*. . . . The Government may regulate corporate political speech through disclaimer and disclosure requirements, but it may not suppress that speech altogether. We turn to the case now before us.

I

A

Citizens United is a nonprofit corporation. It brought this action in the United States District Court for the District of Columbia. A three-judge court later convened to hear the cause. The resulting judgment gives rise to this appeal.

Citizens United has an annual budget of about $12 million. Most of its funds are from donations by individuals; but, in addition, it accepts a small portion of its funds from for-profit corporations.

In January 2008, Citizens United released a film entitled *Hillary: The Movie*. We refer to the film as *Hillary*. It is a 90-minute documentary about then-Senator Hillary Clinton, who was a candidate in the Democratic Party's 2008 Presidential primary elections. *Hillary* mentions Senator Clinton by name and depicts interviews with political commentators and other persons, most of them quite critical of Senator Clinton. *Hillary* was released in theaters and on DVD, but Citizens United wanted to increase distribution by making it available through video-on-demand. . . .

To implement the proposal, Citizens United was prepared to pay for the video-on-demand; and to promote the film, it produced two 10-second ads and one 30-second ad for *Hillary*. Each ad includes a short (and, in our view, pejorative) statement about Senator Clinton, followed by the name of the movie and the movie's Website address. Citizens United desired to promote the video-on-demand offering by running advertisements on broadcast and cable television.

B

Before the Bipartisan Campaign Reform Act of 2002 (BCRA), federal law prohibited—and still does prohibit—corporations and unions from using general treasury funds to make direct contributions to candidates or independent expenditures that expressly advocate the election or defeat of a candidate, through any form of media, in connection with certain qualified federal elections. . . . Corporations and unions are barred from using their general treasury funds for express advocacy or electioneering communications. They may establish, however, a "separate segregated fund" (known as a political action committee, or PAC) for these purposes. The moneys received by the segregated fund are limited to donations from stockholders and employees of the corporation or, in the case of unions, members of the union.

C

Citizens United wanted to make *Hillary* available through video-on-demand within 30 days of the 2008 primary elections. It feared, however, that both the film and the ads would be covered by §441b's ban on corporate-funded independent expenditures, thus subjecting the corporation to civil and criminal penalties under §437g. . . .

II

Before considering whether *Austin* should be overruled, we first address whether Citizens United's claim that §441b cannot be applied to *Hillary* may be resolved on other, narrower grounds. . . .

E

As the foregoing analysis confirms, the Court cannot resolve this case on a narrower ground without chilling political speech, speech that is central to the meaning and purpose of the First Amendment. . . . It is not judicial restraint to accept an unsound, narrow argument just so the Court can avoid another argument with broader implications. Indeed, a court would be remiss in performing its duties were it to accept an unsound principle merely to avoid the necessity of making a broader ruling. Here, the lack of a valid basis for an alternative ruling requires full consideration of the continuing effect of the speech suppression upheld in *Austin*. . . .

III

The First Amendment provides that "Congress shall make no law . . . abridging the freedom of speech." Laws enacted to control or suppress speech may operate at different points in the speech process. . . .

The law before us is an outright ban, backed by criminal sanctions. Section 441b makes it a felony for all corporations—including nonprofit advocacy corporations—either to expressly advocate the election or defeat of candidates or to broadcast electioneering communications within 30 days of a primary election and 60 days of a general election. . . . These prohibitions are classic examples of censorship.

Section 441b is a ban on corporate speech notwithstanding the fact that a PAC created by a corporation can still speak. A PAC is a separate association from the corporation. So the PAC exemption from §441b's expenditure ban, §441b(b)(2), does not allow corporations to speak. Even if a PAC could somehow allow a corporation to speak—and it does not—the option to form PACs does not alleviate the First Amendment problems with §441b. PACs are burdensome alternatives; they are expensive to administer and subject to extensive regulations. . . .

Speech is an essential mechanism of democracy, for it is the means to hold officials accountable to the people. The right of citizens to inquire, to hear, to speak, and to use information to reach consensus is a precondition to enlightened self-government and a necessary means to protect it. The First Amendment "'has its fullest and most urgent application' to speech uttered during a campaign for political office."

For these reasons, political speech must prevail against laws that would suppress it, whether by design or inadvertence. . . .

A

1

The Court has recognized that First Amendment protection extends to corporations. . . .

This protection has been extended by explicit holdings to the context of political speech. Under the rationale of these precedents, political speech does not lose First Amendment protection "simply because its source is a corporation." . . . The Court has thus rejected the argument that political speech of corporations or other associations should be treated differently under the First Amendment simply because such associations are not "natural persons." . . .

B

1

There is simply no support for the view that the First Amendment, as originally understood, would permit the suppression of political speech by media corporations. The Framers may not have anticipated modern business and media corporations. Yet television networks and major newspapers owned by media corporations have become the most important means of mass communication in modern times. The First Amendment was certainly not understood to condone the suppression of political speech in society's most salient media. It was understood as a response to the repression of speech and the press that had existed in England and the heavy taxes on the press that were imposed in the colonies. The great debates between the Federalists and the Anti-Federalists over our founding document were published and expressed in the most important means of mass communication of that era—newspapers owned by individuals. At the founding, speech was open, comprehensive, and vital to society's definition of itself; there were no limits on the sources of speech and knowledge. The Framers may have been unaware of certain types of speakers or forms of communication, but that does not mean that those speakers and media are entitled to less First Amendment protection than those types of speakers and media that provided the means of communicating political ideas when the Bill of Rights was adopted.

Austin interferes with the "open marketplace" of ideas protected by the First Amendment. It permits the Government to ban the political speech of millions of associations of citizens. Most of these are small corporations without large amounts of wealth. This fact belies the Government's argument that the statute is justified on the ground that it prevents the "distorting effects of immense aggregations of wealth." It is not even aimed at amassed wealth.

The censorship we now confront is vast in its reach. The Government has "muffle[d] the voices that best represent the most significant segments of the economy." And "the electorate [has been] deprived of information, knowledge and opinion vital to its function." By suppressing the speech of manifold corporations, both for-profit and nonprofit, the Government prevents their voices and viewpoints from reaching the public and advising voters on which persons or entities are hostile to their interests. Factions will necessarily form in our Republic, but the remedy of "destroying the liberty" of some factions is "worse than the disease." Factions should be checked by permitting them all to speak, and by entrusting the people to judge what is true and what is false.

The purpose and effect of this law is to prevent corporations, including small and nonprofit corporations, from presenting both facts and opinions to the public. This makes *Austin*'s antidistortion rationale all the more an aberration.... Corporate executives and employees counsel Members of Congress and Presidential administrations on many issues, as a matter of routine and often in private. An *amici* brief filed on behalf of Montana and 25 other States notes that lobbying and corporate communications with elected officials occur on a regular basis. When that phenomenon is coupled with §441b, the result is that smaller or nonprofit corporations cannot raise a voice to object when other corporations, including those with vast wealth, are cooperating with the Government. That cooperation may sometimes be voluntary, or it may be at the demand of a Government official who uses his or her authority, influence, and power to threaten corporations to support the Government's policies. Those kinds of interactions are often unknown and unseen. The speech that §441b forbids, though, is public, and all can judge its content and purpose. References to massive corporate treasuries should not mask the real operation of this law. Rhetoric ought not obscure reality.

Even if §441b's expenditure ban were constitutional, wealthy corporations could still lobby elected officials, although smaller corporations may not have the resources to do so. And wealthy individuals and unincorporated associations can spend unlimited amounts on independent expenditures. Yet certain disfavored associations of citizens—those that have taken on the corporate form—are penalized for engaging in the same political speech.

When Government seeks to use its full power, including the criminal law, to command where a person may get his or her information or what distrusted source he or she may not hear, it uses censorship to control thought. This is unlawful. The First Amendment confirms the freedom to think for ourselves. . . .

V

. . . Governments are often hostile to speech, but under our law and our tradition it seems stranger than fiction for our Government to make this political speech a crime. . . .

Some members of the public might consider *Hillary* to be insightful and instructive; some might find it to be neither high art nor a fair discussion on how to set the Nation's course; still others simply might suspend judgment on these points but decide to think more about issues and candidates. Those choices and assessments, however, are not for the Government to make. "The First Amendment underwrites the freedom to experiment and to create in the realm of thought and speech. Citizens must be free to use new forms, and new forums, for the expression of ideas. The civic discourse belongs to the people, and the Government may not prescribe the means used to conduct it."

The judgment of the District Court is reversed with respect to the constitutionality of 2 U. S. C. §441b's restrictions on corporate independent expenditures. The judgment is affirmed with respect to BCRA's disclaimer and disclosure requirements. The case is remanded for further proceedings consistent with this opinion.

It is so ordered.

Acknowledgments

I would like to thank all of the people who have helped bring this series to life by reading drafts, providing edits, and helping to put together the final versions. Aidan Calvelli provided careful editing and thoughtful input on all aspects of the series. Priyanka Podugu brought a keen eye to helping me compile materials, highlighting selections that brought out the key themes of liberty. My wife, Allison Brettschneider, was, as she always is, an invaluable partner in this work, giving substantive editorial feedback. David McNamee, Kevin McGravey, Megan Bird, Olivia Siemens, Amistad Meeks, Noah Klein, and Rakhi Kundra all graciously read drafts and provided valuable comments and suggestions. I would also like to thank Elda Rotor and Elizabeth Vogt from Penguin for all they have done to make this series possible, and Rafe Sagelyn, my agent, for his continued support, encouragement, and guidance.

David McNamee, Kevin McGravey, Megan Bird, Olivia Siemens, Amistad Meeks, Noah Klein, Rakhi Kundra, and Chris Woods all graciously read drafts and provided valuable comments and suggestions.

Unabridged Source Materials

PART I

Calder v. Bull, 3 U.S. 386 (1798)

Marbury v. Madison, 5 U.S. 137 (1803)

PART II

Dred Scott v. Sandford, 60 U.S. 393 (1857)

Yick Wo v. Hopkins, 118 U.S. 356 (1886)

Chae Chan Ping v. United States, 130 U.S. 581 (1889)

Plessy v. Ferguson, 163 U.S. 537 (1896)

United States v. Wong Kim Ark, 169 U.S. 649 (1898)

Korematsu v. United States, 323 U.S. 214 (1944)

Brown v. Board of Education, 347 U.S. 483 (1954)

Cooper v. Aaron, 358 U.S. 1 (1958)

Loving v. Virginia, 388 U.S. 1 (1967)

Plyler v. Doe, 457 U.S. 202 (1982)

Gratz v. Bollinger, 539 U.S. 244 (2003)

Grutter v. Bollinger, 539 U.S. 306 (2003)

PART III

Schenck v. United States, 249 U.S. 47 (1919)

Brandenburg v. Ohio, 395 U.S. 444 (1969)

Tinker v. Des Moines Independent Community School District, 393 U.S. 503 (1969)

New York Times Company v. United States, 403 U.S. 713 (1971)

PART IV

Griswold v. Connecticut, 381 U.S. 479 (1965)

Roe v. Wade, 410 U.S. 113 (1973)

Planned Parenthood v. Casey, 505 U.S. 833 (1992)

Dobbs v. Jackson Women's Health Organization # U.S. # (2022)

PART V

Bowers v. Hardwick, 478 U.S. 186 (1986)

Romer v. Evans, 517 U.S. 620 (1996)

Lawrence v. Texas, 539 U.S. 558 (2003)

Obergefell v. Hodges, 576 U.S. __ (2015)

PART VI

Baker v. Carr, 369 U.S. 186 (1961)

Reynolds v. Sims, 377 U.S. 533 (1964)

Shaw v. Reno, 509 U.S. 630 (1993)

Citizens United v. Federal Election Commission, 558 U.S. 310 (2010)

ON IMPEACHMENT

The Presidency on Trial

On Impeachment provides key historic writings to understand impeachment and learn about three presidents who have been subject to the process.

RELIGIOUS FREEDOM

To understand issues around religious liberty, this volume provides ideas from the United States' founding to the present day and key U.S. Supreme Court judgements to ask how the two twin pillars of religious freedom—free exercise and the limit on religious establishment—unfold in daily life.